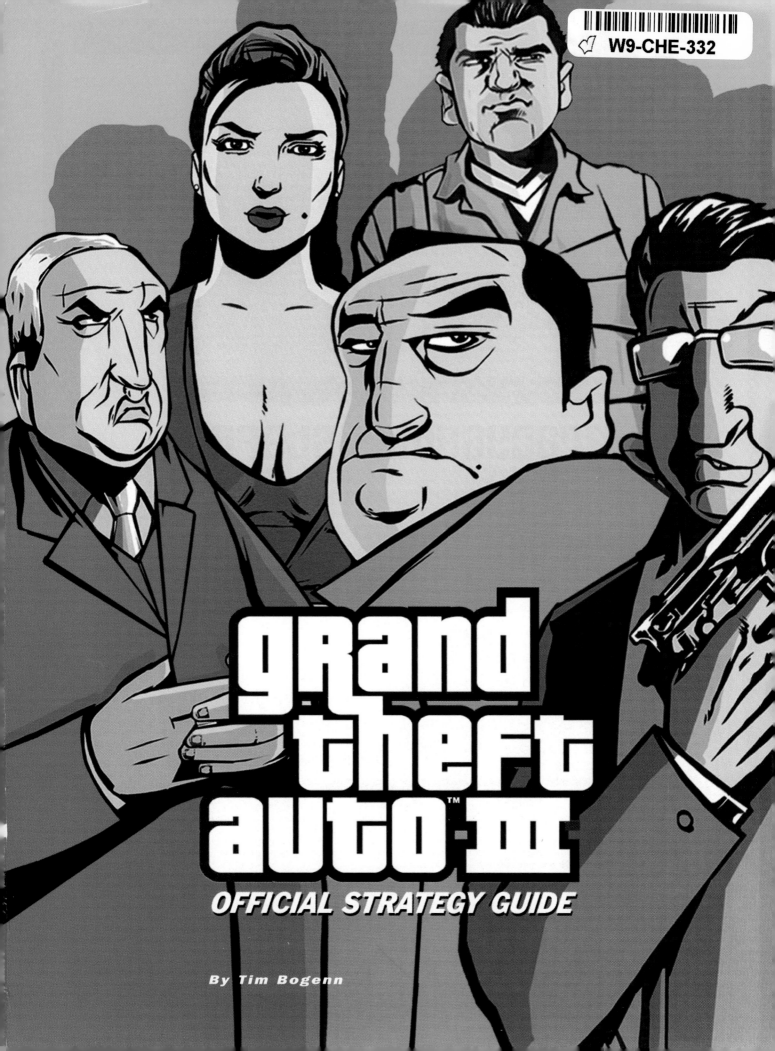

grand theft auto™ III

OFFICIAL STRATEGY GUIDE

By Tim Bogenn

GRAND THEFT AUTO III®
OFFICIAL STRATEGY GUIDE

BRADYGAMES STAFF

DIRECTOR OF PUBLISHING
DAVID WAYBRIGHT

EDITOR-IN-CHIEF
H. LEIGH DAVIS

CREATIVE DIRECTOR
ROBIN LASEK

MARKETING MANAGER
JANET ESHENOUR

LICENSING ASSISTANT
MIKE DEGLER

ASSISTANT MARKETING MANAGER
SUSIE NIEMAN

CREDITS

SENIOR PROJECT EDITOR
DAVID B. BARTLEY

SCREENSHOT EDITOR
MICHAEL OWEN

BOOK DESIGNER
CAROL ANN STAMILE

PRODUCTION DESIGNER
BOB KLUNDER

ACKNOWLEDGEMENTS

I would like to thank everyone at the Rockstar/Take 2 New York office for making me feel at home for the three weeks I spent in the middle of your offices! I would especially like to thank the following people: Sam Houser, Laura Paterson, Jeremy Pope, Adam Davidson, Jenefer Gross, Terry Donovan, and Jamie Leece. Without your day to day assistance, this could not have been possible. Thank you one and all.

It was pretty surreal playing GTA3 in the Big Apple while creating complete havoc in Liberty City. Unfortunately, the World Trade Towers were attacked the following week and I was forced to leave virtual reality rather abruptly and deal with a whole new reality. My deepest condolences to those who have lost loved ones.

A big thanks goes to my lovely wife, Jennifer, who had to pull both our duties at home during my stay in NY—thanks and I love you.

Rockstar and DMA, your hard work and attention to detail in every facet have come beaming through GTA3! Congratulations on such an enjoyable game.

2

WELCOME TO LIBERTY CITY WHERE SECURITY IS CHEAP AT ANY PRICE

TABLE OF CONTENTS

INTRODUCTION 4
CHAPTER 1: GAME BASICS 6
    Power-up/Location Maps 14
LIBERTY CITY MAPS 16
CHAPTER 2: PORTLAND 20
    Intro 21
    Luigi Goterelli 24
    Joey Leone 31
    Toni Cipriani 36
    Salvatore Leone 39
    Toni Cipriani (cont.) .39
    Salvatore Leone (cont.) 41
INDUSTRIAL DISTRICT EXTRA MISSIONS 46
    El Burro 46
EXTRA MISSIONS .50
    Marty Chonks 50
    RC TOYZ 53
    4x4 53
CHAPTER 3: STAUNTON ISLAND 54
    Asuka Kasen 56
    Kenji Kasen 62
    Ray Machowski 68
    Donald Love 72
STAUNTON ISLAND EXTRA MISSIONS 75
    King Courtney 75
    RC TOYZ 78
    4X4 79
CHAPTER 4: SHORESIDE VALE 80
    Donald Love 82
    Asuka Kasen (Construction Site) 87
    Ray Machowski 94
    Catalina 95
SHORESIDE VALE EXTRA MISSIONS 100
    D-Ice (Hoods) 100
    4x4 104
    RC TOYZ 104
CHAPTER 5: SECRETS 105
    Hidden Package Maps 110

introduction

Grand Theft Auto III takes place in Liberty City—a completely unique universe with its own laws, standards, ethics, and morals (or lack thereof).

There are dozens of ways to take out the inhabitants—punches, kicks, head butts, baseball bats, handguns, Uzis, AK-47s, shotguns, M-16s, sniper rifles, rocket launchers, grenades, Molotov cocktails, and flame-throwers.

You must work your way through the pecking-order of the gangs, receive better jobs and eventually meet, use, and extinguish bigger bosses. However, there is an opposing force that will try to thwart your objectives (harmful as they may be). Liberty City's law enforcement includes cops, SWAT Teams, FBI agents, and the Army. They all work cooperatively to keep Liberty City moderately protected and acceptably corrupt.

Liberty City is divided into three districts: Portland, Staunton Island, and Shoreside Vale. Each has its own look and feel—with different styles of buildings, cars, and inhabitants. Bridges, subways, and tunnels connect these three areas. If one of those options can't get you there, you can take a boat across the bay and dock in the next district.

There are hundreds of pedestrians throughout Liberty City, each with their own unpredictable characteristics. Businessmen hustle to work, bums get in the way, gang members look for trouble, and hookers prowl for business. These characters act and react to situations and the activity surrounding them in their own unique way. Even if you did nothing but walk the streets meddling in the affairs of its citizens, you would still be blissfully submerged into the Liberty City universe!

But that, indeed, is not all you will be doing. You're going to get involved on a much more active level.

Let the crime wave begin!

4

CHAPTER

1

GAME BASICS

CONTROLS

There are two basic sets of controls for the two primary planes of your existence—in your car and out of your car. What else is there?!

OUT-OF-CAR CONTROLS (SETUP 1)

L1	Look Forward
L2	Cycle Weapon Left
R1	Target
R2	Cycle Weapon Right
D-Pad	Movement
L Analog Stick	Movement
R Analog Stick	First Person Camera Look Behind R3
Select	Camera Modes
Start	Pause
Triangle	Enter Vehicles
Circle	Attack or Fire weapon
X	Run
Square	Jump

IN-CAR CONTROLS (SETUP 1)

L1	Change Radio Stations
L2	Look Left
L3	Horn
L2 + R2	Look Behind
R1	Hand Brake
R2	Look Right
D-Pad	Vehicle Steering
L Analog Stick	Vehicle Steering
R Analog Stick	Turret Control/Special Mission Trigger R3
Select	Camera Modes
Start	Pause
Triangle	Exit Vehicle
Circle	Car Weapon
X	Accelerate
Square	Brake or Reverse

saving your game
Hideouts

Your Hideout appears on the radar as a small, green house icon in each of the three major districts. As soon as you enter a new district, only that district's Hideout will appear on the radar.

To save your progress, you'll enter a changing room, elevator, or apartment foyer. You can save your game only when you are NOT working on a mission, just as you cannot take a second job while working on another.

Your Hideout is always near a large garage, which will make it possible for you to park and save a car with your game save. As you progress to new districts, you are incrementally allowed more cars to save. To do this, drive a vehicle in, then exit the garage and save by entering the Hideout door—follow the house icon. Keep in mind that saving your progress will advance the clock by six hours.

Refuge and Repair
There are other advantages to returning to your Hideout. When you park a damaged car in the garage, exit the vehicle, and close the garage door, the car will be repaired. Also, if you've been collecting Hidden Packages, you can unlock power-ups that will frequently regenerate at your Hideout!

Getting wasted or busted
Hospitals: wasted!

This is where you end up if you try to swim with the fishes by geting shot up, blown up, run over, roughed up too much or, in short, 'Wasted.' You'll always be taken to the closest hospital where they will stitch your remains back together and replenish your Health to 100%. On the downside, it will cost you $1000, which is automatically deducted from your account to cover the medical bills. On top of that, they take all of your weapons! Any mission you were currently working through will be 'Failed.'

Health Tips
Enter an ambulance when injured and receive 20 points of Health. You can always find a couple Heart power-ups outside the hospitals in Liberty City. Check out the Hooker cheat in the Secrets chapter for bonus health!

Game Basics

POLICE STATIONS: BUSTED!

When you're arrested, you'll be sent to the nearest police station where the cops will then take $400 in bribery money and all your weapons. Also, any current mission will be 'Failed.' You must be pulled out of a vehicle and have a Wanted Level to get arrested; otherwise, the cops will just kill you and you'll be sent to the hospital. So, if you see a cop opening your car door, put the pedal to the metal!

WANTED LEVEL

The row of six stars in the top-right corner of the screen indicates your level of bad behavior. If you do nothing to calm the authorities and only antagonize them further, your Wanted Level increases and greater forces are sent after you.

When additional backup is called, the previous authorities on the scene do not throw in the towel and go for donuts. For example, in a Wanted Level of 6, you can expect to see LCPD, SWAT Enforcers, FBI, and the Army with a Tank and two helicopters!

WANTED LEVEL	REPERCUSSIONS
1	LCPD Level 1
2	LCPD Level 2
3	SWAT Level 1 & a Helicopter
4	SWAT Level 2
5	FBI
6	Army & Second Helicopter

BREAKING THE LAW

If you run over, shoot, or punch a cop, your Wanted Level will increase. If you try to steal a police car while a cop is still in it, the heat will be all over you. Simply targeting a cop with a gun without firing the weapon is cause for a Wanted Level. Yep, they saw that! If you steal a car, shoot someone, or start a rumble while a cop is watching, you will become Wanted. Also, just bumping a police car hard enough to spill his coffee will get your face in the post offices.

DECREASING YOUR WANTED LEVEL

There are just a few ways to reduce your Wanted Level. You can lay low, make yourself scarce, and get out of sight for a period of time. This works with Levels 1 & 2. For higher levels, you can go to Pay 'n' Spray to get rid of all the levels. Just don't try to paint over a law enforcement vehicle—they just don't take 'em that hot!

To bring the levels down one at a time, you can find the 'Police Bribes' scattered throughout Liberty City. These are the blue and white star icons found in alleyways and other hidden places. There's one in the alley a block away from the Police Station in Portland, conveniently placed there in case you steal some wheels right in front of the cops after getting Busted.

8

RUNNING

To run, hold down the X button and control your character in any direction. Sooner or later, your character will become exhausted and slow to a walk once again. If you just stop on the spot and allow him to catch his breath, he'll recover quicker than if you continue running (slowly).

exercise

The more you run, the more endurance you build up—just like exercise puts you in better shape in real life. So, when your not on a mission and looking for items and stuff, try huffing it instead of taking a car and you'll see the advantages in the long run.

action tips

shooting

Use the R2 and L2 buttons to cycle through your weapons. Press the Circle button to shoot the weapon, hold the R1 button for targeting, and switch targets by simultaneously pressing the R2 or L2 buttons. The button you choose depends on the direction of the next target.

Street Shots	POLICE REPORT
	☐ PRIMARY ☐ SUPP PAGE _____

Beware that any shooting in the city will attract law enforcement.

running while shooting

Hold down on the R1 targeting button to remain locked onto targets while running and shooting. Turn your back toward the locked target to reach around and shoot behind yourself!

There are only a few weapons that you can hold and run at your normal speed. The Handgun, Uzi, Grenades, and Molotov Cocktails can be held while still achieving maximum running speed. Some weapons can be used only while standing still. The Rocket Launcher, Flame-thrower, Sniper Rifle, and M-16 cannot be fired while you are walking or running.

drive-by shooting

Enter any car with the Uzi selected and press L2 + ● or R2 + ● to fire. Your character will reach his arm out the window and fire! The shoulder determines which direction you fire. Control your aim by moving forward and backward with your vehicle.

driving

The Handbrake's default assignment is the R1 button. This is a much more useful brake than the regular brake (Square) for the style of driving that you'll be doing. Using the Handbrake in conjunction with sharp turning maneuvers will allow you to powerslide around corners. The regular brake will only slow you down and force you to take wider, slower turns. However, using both brakes together is often necessary when you're going too fast for a turn. If you're speeding through town and need to whip around a corner without flipping, first depress the normal brake, then add the handbrake, and then turn. The result should be a sharp, controlled powerslide turn.

car jacking

Don't try this at home, kids! Stand in front of the moving vehicle to make it stop, then face it and press the Triangle button. As soon as you enter the car, press on the Reverse or Gas forward Buttons to keep the driver from pulling you back out of the vehicle. When chasing after a car, hold down the Run button while pressing the Triangle button as you get closer to initiate the jacking.

game basics

fast cars

You can always count on the local gangs to have the fastest cars. If you need one at the beginning of the game and you're nowhere near the Banshee at the Easy Credit Autos dealership, then the next best thing is a Mafia Sentinel or a Diablo Stallion. When you reach Staunton Island, you'll find that the Asian gangs have the best cars. The Yakuza Stinger is a fine automobile; much better than the Yardie Lobo. However, there are also nicer areas of town where the business people drive Cheetahs, Banshees, Stingers, and the coveted Infernus!

car radio

Each vehicle is tuned to its own radio station, playing a combination of licensed tracks, specially created music, and talk radio. Press the L1 button down to change the station.

when to bail out

It's very important to know when to bail out of a vehicle. Regardless of the condition of your car, even if it's brand spanking new, it's going to eventually explode if it overturns and remains upside-down! Press the Triangle button repeatedly as the vehicle is turning over (and when you know it won't flip back onto its wheels) to exit as soon as possible—usually when the vehicle is completely stationary.

stats menu

The in-game Statistics Menu is huge! It tracks everything! Check this menu frequently to see where you stand as a criminal and to keep track of... well, just about everything. Most of the categories are self explanatory, but there are a few you may question. The following is a brief description of those more confusing categories.

MENU CATEGORY	DESCRIPTION
Helicopters Destroyed	Tally of helicopters you destroy with the M-16 or Rocket Launcher.
Kgs of Explosives Used	Kgs are Grenades. This stat shows the number you've used.
Unique Jumps Completed	There are 20 Insane Stunt Challenges scattered throughout Liberty City; this will track these completed jumps.
Pickups Found	This refers to the 100 Hidden Packages that are peppered all over Liberty City.

BLOOD MONEY

Most pedestrians drop cash when killed. You can also earn $1-25 for car collisions and $50 for car explosions!

10

Items

Armor

When you find one of these charms, an Armor Meter appears near your Health Meter in the top-right corner of the screen. Your armor will absorb the damage done to you. You begin with 100 maximum. When this is depleted, damage is taken off your Health Meter as it did before you found the Armor power-up. There are five in Portland, five in Staunton Island, but only four in Shoreside Vale.

Health

Mostly found around hospitals, these will regenerate over time. These power-ups restore your Health to a maximum of 100. If you aren't hurt, you won't be able to pick them up. There are 12 in Portland, 12 in Staunton Island, and eight in Shoreside Vale.

Adrenaline

These little drug power-ups give you super human fighting abilities. Pick one up and then punch someone to see what we mean! There are five in Portland, four in Staunton Island, and five in Shoreside Vale.

Hidden Packages

There are 100 Packages hidden throughout Liberty City. Each Package earns you $1,000! Collect them in 10s and power-ups begin to continually regenerate at your Hideouts. There are 33 in Portland, 36 in Staunton Island, and 31 in Shoreside Vale. See *Chapter 5: Secrets* for the locations of all 100 Packages on our Liberty City Maps!

Police Bribes

Each shield icon you pass through will reduce your Wanted Level by one. Bribe the Police and you can get away with murder—literally! There are eight in Portland, 10 in Staunton Island, and six in Shoreside Vale.

Rampages

Run into one of these skull icons, when you're not currently involved in a current mission, to begin a Rampage Challenge. You'll have an alotted amount of time to destroy a certain number of objects or gang members. Succeed and you win some dough; fail and each package moves to a second location. Fail again and they will all move back to their original locations, and so on. There are six in Portland, seven in Staunton Island, and seven in Shoreside Vale.

Weapons

Weapon power-ups can found in various locations and don't require you to loot the slain. These weapons have unlimited ammo caches. Portland is home to nine such power-ups, but no Rocket Launcher, M-16, or Sniper Rifle varieties. There are eight Weapon power-ups in Staunton Island and nine more in Shoreside Vale—and they're all good!

Baseball Bat

These are used for the business of clubbing thugs, rather than for sport!

Handgun (Colt 45)

You can't walk down a Liberty City street without tripping over one of these guns. This light, semi-automatic weapon gives you the ability to run and shoot at the same time. Don't leave home without it.

UZI

This rapid-fire machine gun is far more damaging than the Colt 45, and can also be fired while running. It maintains fair performance at long range.

SHOTGUN

This pump-action weapon is inappropriate for long distance targeting, but is the best choice for up-close and personal carnage. You cannot run and shoot with this weapon.

MOLOTOV COCKTAIL

This explosive device serves up a gasoline-filled bottle with a rag stuffed in the top. The poor man's grenade is best used for your torching needs. Press and hold the Shoot button longer to toss the cocktail further.

GRENADE

Although it's much more sophisticated on the evolutionary scale of things than the Molotov Cocktail, it still serves the same general purpose—with quicker results. Use the same button technique as described with the Molotov Cocktail to gauge the distance of your throw.

AK-47

Designed by Mikhail Timofeyevich Kalashnikov, this weapon fires rounds faster than the Uzi, and is more deadly and accurate at longe range. You cannot run and shoot with this weapon.

M-16

A United States weapon, the M-16 was created at Johns Hopkins University in September 1948 for the purpose of increasing the effectiveness of military operations. This weapon is very powerful and will take out vehicles in a flash flurry of bullets. It uses a sight and you'll feel the recoil as it's fired. You cannot run and shoot with this weapon.

SNIPER RIFLE

This is the appropriate weapon for difficult missions. It uses a zooming sight for precision and is able to dispatch enemies with deadly accuracy from great distances. Use this weapon when you don't want to attract attention.

FLAME-THROWER

The German Army first began experimenting with flame-throwers in 1900. You can continue the tradition in the 21st century in Liberty City. The flame-thrower uses nitrogen to force oil through the nozzle. Ignited by a small charge, the oil becomes a stream of fire. You can't run and fire this weapon and you wouldn't want to even if you could.

ROCKET LAUNCHER

This shoulder mounted weapon fires a small fin-stabilized, rocket-propelled grenade. Pulling the trigger releases an electric current that will ignite the ammunition's rocket stage. Short-range ignition is suicidal. This weapon uses a fixed sight and has a safety lock when not supported correctly for firing.

THE MAIN PLAYERS

8-BALL

Your comrade in crime is a bomb expert and franchise owner of 8-Ball's Autoyard, a facility that offers car accessories and upgrades. After escaping the shackles of the law, he was able to get back into business. Nobody's buisness!

LUIGI GOTERELLI

If you gotta climb da ladder of crime, you might as well start with the lowest rung. Luigi Goterelli runs a strip joint in Portland, the Sex Club 7, for the Mafia. It's nothing more than a front to pimp the ladies to the more affluent clients.

JOEY LEONE

The Don's only living son, Joey owns a garage in Trenton where he only services the finest stolen vehicles. His despise for the Forelli Brothers and love for hitting the banks will keep you plenty busy—and with a name like Leone, it's got to get you somewhere.

TONI CIPRIANI

Toni Cipriani is the Mob's number one extortionist, debt collector, and... well, a mama's boy. If you need to see Toni, he can always be found at Mamma Cipriani's restaurant in St Mark's. Get involved with Toni and you'll be an instant 'hit' at any Triad parties!

SALVATORE LEONE

The Don, the Mafia's big cheese. If you are the best at being bad and can get jobs from Salvatore, you'll certainly see some serious green, but with the job comes grave uncertainty that you may not live to enjoy the wealth. With the war brewing with the Colombian Cartel and the ongoing skirmishes with the Triads, you'd better get life insurance with your earnings.

ASUKA KASEN

Born into the Yakuza crime syndicate, Asuka proves she can run with the toughest of them. However, to earn her trust you must bite the hand that feeds you. That may not prove to be so puzzling when you discover that the hand wants you dead.

KENJI KASEN

Owner of Kenji's Casino in Torrington, member of the Yakuza crime syndicate, and brother to Asuka Kasen, Kenji Kasen has a lot to lose if the Colombian Cartel push SPANK in Staunton Island. Rub elbows with Kenji and you'll be thrown back into the war that you thought you left back in Portland.

DONALD LOVE

Playboy millionaire, Donald Love, CEO of Love Media, has a skeleton in his closet and he visits it frequently! Taking jobs from him is a no-brainer, but look closely at your reward because Donald's hobby is counterfeiting.

POWER-UP/ LOCATION MAPS

Staunton Island

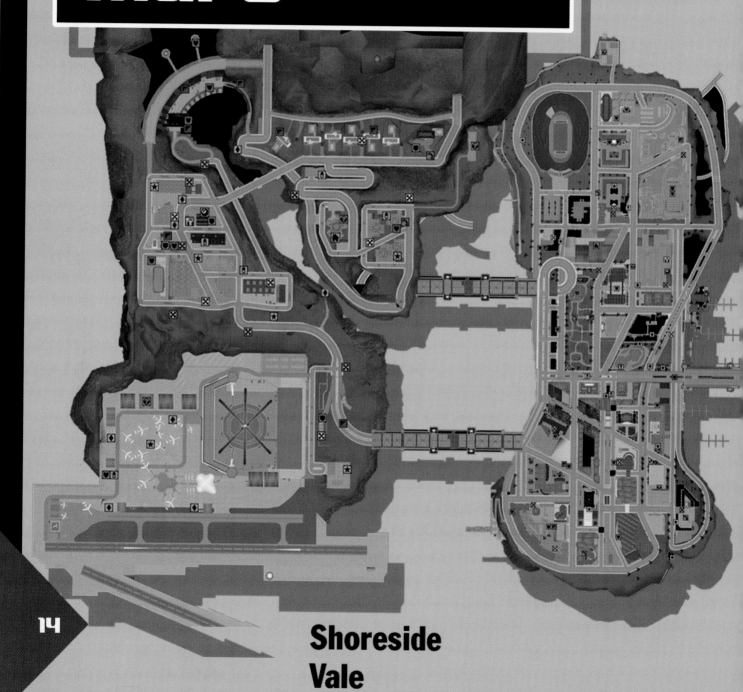

Shoreside Vale

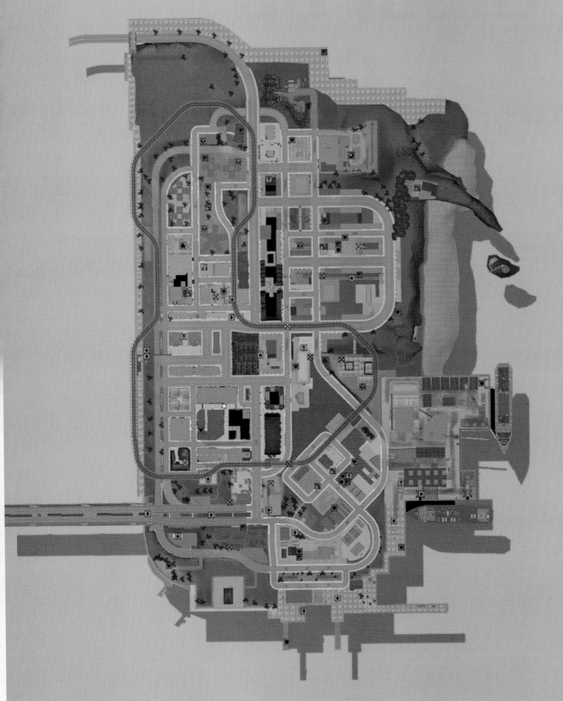

Weapon:
Health:
Armour:
Rampage:
Safehouse:
Mission Contact:
Sprayshop:
Bombshop:
Adrenaline:
Police Bribe:
Unique Stunt:
Secret Vehicles:

Portland

LiBerty City maps

PORTLAND

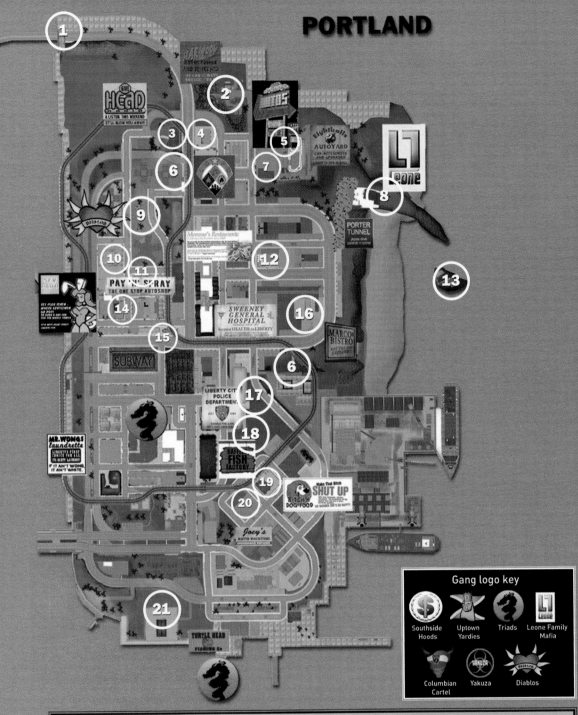

Gang logo key

Southside Hoods | Uptown Yardies | Triads | Leone Family Mafia

Columbian Cartel | Yakuza | Diablos

1	Porter Tunnel	11	Pay 'n' Spray
2	Car Crusher	12	Toni's (Momma's Restaurant)
3	Head Radio	13	Portland Rock
4	Harwood Fire Station	14	Luigi's Sex Club 7
5	8-Ball's Autoyard	15	Portland Subway
6	El-Train Station (3)	16	Marco's Bistro
7	Capitol Autos Dealership	17	Sweeney General Hospital
8	Salvatore's Mansion	18	LCPD
9	El Burro Contact Point	19	Marty Chonk's Bitch 'n' Dog Food
10	Portland Hideout	20	Joey Leone's Garage
		21	Triad's (Turtle Head Fish Factory)

CITY maps

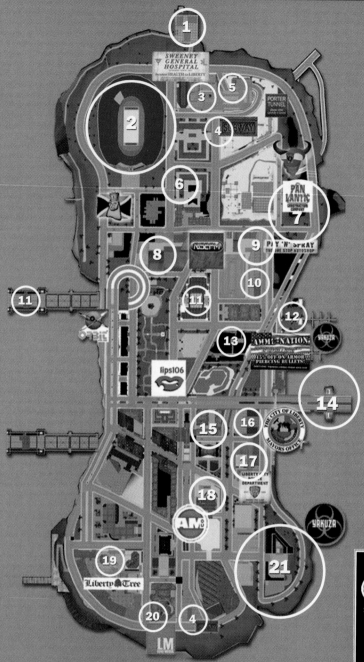

STAUNTON ISLAND

Gang logo key

| Southside Hoods | Uptown Yardies | Triads | Leone Family Mafia |
| Columbian Cartel | Yakuza | Diablos |

1	Phil Cassidy's Army Surplus	12	Asuka's Condo
2	Liberty Memorial Coliseum	13	AmmuNation
3	Sweeney General Hospital	14	Callahan Bridge
4	Subways (2)	15	FBI
5	Porter Tunnel, Rockford Slipway	16	City Hall (Mayor O'Donovan)
6	King Courtney Contact Point	17	LCPD Head Quarters
7	Pan-Lantic Construction	18	AMco Head Quarters
8	Staunton Island Hideout	19	Liberty Tree Offices
9	Pay 'n' Spray	20	Love Media (Donald Love)
10	8-Ball's Bomb Shop	21	Kenji's Casino
11	Shopping Mall		

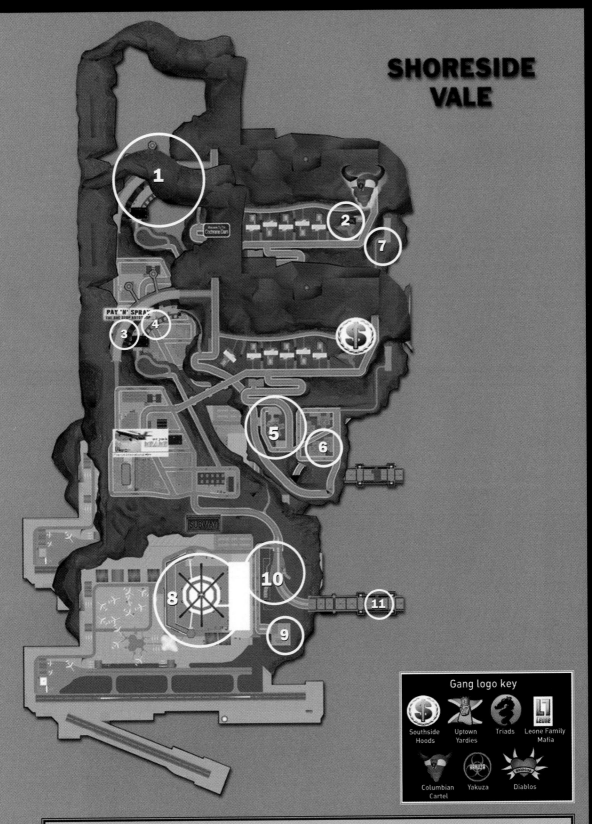

SHORESIDE VALE

Gang logo key

Southside Hoods	
Uptown Yardies	
Triads	
Leone Family Mafia	
Columbian Cartel	
Yakuza	
Diablos	

1	Cochrane Dam	7	Staunton View Picnic Area
2	Colombian Cartel Mansion	8	Francis International Airport
3	Pay 'n' Spray	9	Airport Subway Station
4	8-Ball's Bomb Shop	10	Porter Tunnel (Francis Slipway)
5	Shoreside Hideout	11	Shoreside Lift Bridge
6	D-Ice Contact Point		

20

CHAPTER

2

INDUSTRIAL PORTLAND

introduction

Relax! This game is like no other. It redefines what gaming should be. It's funny and fun, beautiful and dirty—you won't want to put the controller down for months. GTA 3 features many (and sometimes endless) adrenalized Missions, including the never-ending Side Missions for the Taxi, Ambulance, Police Car, Firetruck, and Vigilante.

If your goal is to play all the missions, it's best to stick with each contact until all of his or her jobs have been exhausted, then move on to the next contact. You can actually skip what seem like major missions and still progress through the entire game. As long as you keep making contacts through your current boss and moving up the crime ladder, you'll progress. If you need extra dough to cover weapons or bodywork for a difficult job, take some little jobs to fatten your wallet. This guide covers it all, so you won't miss a thing!

more Than one way to skin a cat

Use your imagination. GTA 3 is a very complex game, so always remember that there are many ways to accomplish the rudiments of each mission. If you are given a grenade and asked to destroy a vehicle, this doesn't mean that all the other ways to demolish a vehicle are now thrown out the window.

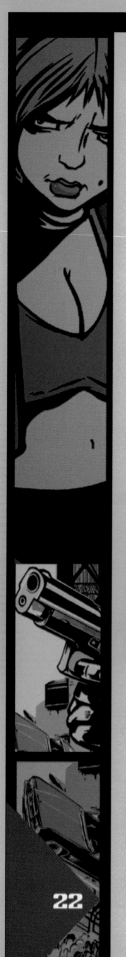

PORTLAND

GIVE ME LIBERTY: INTRODUCTION MISSION

After your assisted breakout from the transport vehicle, your ex-con friend, 8-Ball, describes a place in the Red Light District where the two of you can lay low. His hands are bandaged and he can't drive, so it's up to you. Enter the getaway car (a Karuma) and familiarize yourself with the driving controls as you exit Callahan Bridge, then make your way into the Industrial District

Damaged Bridge!	POLICE REPORT
	☐ PRIMARY ☐ SUPP PAGE _____

The Callahan Bridge needs major repairs. Don't attempt to jump it or you'll end up in the river, and then the hospital—except in the beginning of the game when you'll start from the beginning once again. This bridge will be repaired as you complete this district's dirty jobs.

Play with the different camera angles (defaulted to the Select button) to find one that best suits you. There's a Chopper-cam view that will remind veteran Grand Theft Auto players of the previous games!

IN-GAME TIPS

Pay very close attention to the helpful tips that appear in the top-left corner of the screen as you delve into new experiences. With all the action and things to watch for, these tips often disappear before you can read them—good thing you have this guide!

The radar in the bottom-left corner of the screen always registers target mission destinations with a colored blip. Drive toward the red blip on the radar to find an alley where the two of you can change clothes and learn about the game saving feature.

AUTOMOTIVE CARE

Even though it's a game and it's fun to smash into things, try to take it easy on your car. If it starts billowing smoke badly, fire quickly follows. After that, BOOM! Bye-bye car and bye-bye life. Losing this car in the first mission places you back on Callahan Bridge to start over; later you'll end up at the nearest hospital.

Watch the bottom-right corner of the screen as you jump into cars and enter new areas. The display will indicate car and district names. When you see "Red Light District" appear, you are close to the first destination. Here, in a wide alley, a blue light beam (Blue Marker) emits from the ground. This is the same spot indicated on the radar.

You and 8-Ball get out of the car and duck into a building to change into civilian clothes. Find the Information icons near the doors. Walk into them and learn the basics of saving your progress and how to guarantee that you have a car to drive off in after loading a saved game. These Information icons appear all around town, and they'll help you understand certain gameplay mechanics.

THE HIDEOUT:
SAVING YOUR PROGRESS

If you'd like to save your progress, return to this Hideout and enter the door that you just exited after changing your clothes. You can only save your game when you are NOT working on a mission, just as you cannot take a second job while working on another. The large garage next to the save room will save one car with your game save. To do this, drive one vehicle in, then exit the garage and save by entering the smaller door. Keep in mind that saving your progress will advance the clock by six hours.

Before returning to the vehicle, take the bat near the ramp that's basking in a red glow and give it a few swings with the Circle button. To put the bat away and go back to fists, press L2 or R2.

Get in the car and go find 8-Ball's boss, Luigi. Why not? You're free and you need to earn a living, right? Follow the blip on the radar a few blocks down the direction you just came from and stop in the Blue Marker. Use the Handbrake—it's a quicker, more reliable stop. The regular brake is also the reverse gear and you can end up rocking on and off the mark.

DRIVING MADMAN

Don't worry about running red lights or driving over medians, even when the police are present. This will not cause the Wanted Level to register even the slightest bit. Hey, this is Liberty City, what do you expect?! You can also run people over for Stat points, but avoid doing this when the cops are around.

In a cinematic, your character and 8-Ball go through the alley to a service door in the back of the Sex Club 7. This is the introduction to Luigi. During the Luigi missions, you'll be introduced to Joey, but stick to the Luigi missions until you've finished all of his jobs.

LUIGI GOTERELLI
LUIGI 1: LUIGI'S GIRL

PAYOFF: $1500
JOB DESCRIPTION: Luigi wants you to steal a car, pick up one of his girls, Misty, from the clinic (classy!) and bring her back to this location... untouched!

If the car you arrived in is not smoking, then jump in and head toward the blip on the radar. If the car is not to your criminal liking, then grab something nearby that interests you.

Car Handling
Notice that the different vehicles in the game handle like their real life counterparts. A van will drive heavy and sluggish, while a sedan will be quicker with a lower center of gravity.

There are usually plenty of taxis in this area. To hitch a ride, just walk up to the driver or passenger's side and press the Triangle button.

Auto-Matic Theft Tracking

You don't have to be too close to a vehicle to initiate the entry maneuver. You can actually track moving vehicles by pressing the Triangle button as the car approaches, and then catch up with the car (by using the X button) as it slows at a stop sign or hits slower traffic.

Be Careful When You Jack!

POLICE REPORT
☐ PRIMARY ☐ SUPP PAGE _____

Be aware that the driver you pull from a vehicle may not be all that pleased that you are stealing his or her car. If you don't take off soon after the jacking, the driver is liable to re-enter the car and throw YOU out! Also, criminals and gangsters are usually packing heat and will open fire on you!

Misty will appear as a green blip on the radar. Head toward the blip through Chinatown and St. Mark's. Pick her up in Portland View—she's standing outside Sweeney General Hospital under the shelter.

Merging Into Traffic

Use the L2 and R2 buttons while in a vehicle to view the left and right sides. This is a good practice to get into while pulling back out onto the street because it minimizes the chances of a mission-compromising accident.

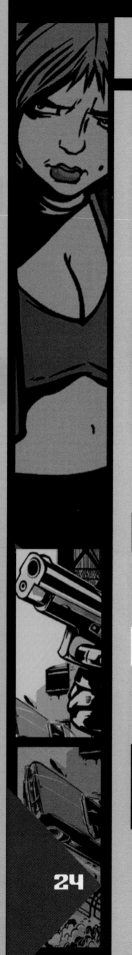

HOSPItaL: WaSteD!

This is where you end up if you get roughed up too much, a.k.a. "Wasted." Sweeney General is where you go when you bite it in the Industrial District. To learn more about being Wasted, check out the *Chapter 1: Game Basics*.

Heart Power-UPS

There are two Heart icons just up the ramp and to the left as you face the front door of Sweeney General Hospital.

POLice Station: BUSteD!

When arrested, the cops take $400 in bribery money and seize your entire arsenal of weapons. To learn more about being "Busted," your Wanted Level, and the repercussions when these levels increase, look in *Chapter 1: Game Basics*.

Head back to Luigi's club in the Red Light District using the blip on the radar to guide you. Stop in the Blue Marker to complete the misson and collect $1500. Who says a life of crime doesn't pay? Well, we'll see.

TaXi MiSSiOnS

If you're in a Taxi after dropping off Misty, you can begin the Taxi Missions by pressing the R3 button. To learn more about these and other never-ending side missions, see *Chapter 1: Game Basics*. You can also start the Police Car and Ambulance missions at this time.

After finishing Luigi's first job, the second will not occur until you visit him once again.

"L" FOr LUiGi

The letter "L" appears on the radar over Luigi's club between missions. This is a reminder that Luigi is there and has jobs waiting for you. The letter will not disappear until after you complete every one of his jobs.

Head to the alley beside the Sex Club 7 to find another Blue Marker. Step into the glow to accept Luigi's next job.

LUiGi 2: DOn't SPanKa Ma BitCH UP

PAYOFF: $2000

JOB DeSCriPtiOn: Clobber SPANK pusher in Portland Harbor with a bat, then take his car and respray it.

A bat appears across the street as you leave the alley. Take it, then take a ride. Follow the blip on the radar to Portland Harbor.

WEAPON COLLECTION

If you need a weapon, you must first exit a vehicle to pick it up. You cannot run through a weapon while in a car to obtain it.

As you drive to Portland Harbor, be wary that all roads and routes are not mapped on the radar. When you appear to be close to the blip, look around for shortcuts that'll take you closer—through alleys, parks, or whatever. You don't need to stick to the roads; the cops don't care, so why should you?

Drive down the gradient slope to enter the Portland Docks. Continue to plow through the crowds as you make your way north toward the blip on the radar representing the pusher with the SPANK.

As you near the SPANKers, a cinema will show the pusher with two hookers. Drive up close, get out of the car, then pull out the bat and let the wiseguy approach you. As he does, introduce the bat to his face. Ouch! It's not crucial to the mission to avoid hitting the hookers. Keep nailing the guy while he's down until the pavement is painted crimson.

Enter the Stallion and head for the Body Shop indicated by the orange blip on the radar. Be careful not to destroy the car—it's irreplaceable. If it blows up, you fail the mission, so drive carefully.

The Pay 'n' Spray Auto Shop is very close to Luigi's club in the Red Light District. Enter the corner shop and pull into the garage. This first bit of bodywork is free, but from now on it will cost you a thousand dollars for each paint job.

With a fresh coat of paint, take the Stallion to an alley in Portland View directly across the entrance to the Sweeney Hospital and pull it into the garage that opens as you drive into the Blue Marker. Exit the vehicle and collect on the job. A cool two grand! Steal some wheels and return to Luigi's for more work.

LUIGI 3: DRIVE MISTY FOR ME

PAYOFF: $1000

JOB DESCRIPTION: Pick up Misty from Hepburn Heights, then drive her over to Joey's garage in Trenton.

JOEY JOBS

Upon completion of this mission, you'll be able to do jobs for the Don's kid, Joey. However, we suggest that you finish out the rest of Luigi's jobs before inquiring into Joey's business.

Find a car just in front of the Sex Club 7 and head north without turning off the street. Hepburn Heights is just a few blocks down the road. Misty is waiting in a parking lot on the right.

When you reach the Blue Marker, honk the horn (L3 button) to let Misty know you're there. When she gets in the car, head toward the new new blip on the radar. If you are drawn to Portland View, you'll see that you must go just past the police station, east of the road across a grassy field. Hurdle the curb and cross the field to enter Trenton. The Blue Marker is just around the first block, in front of Joey's Garage.

Misty imparts some sweet talk and a hug, then enters the garage. Joey says he's heard good things about you from Luigi and if you return later, he (Joey) will be able to hook you up with some more work.

That was a quickie—and you made an easy $1000!

"J" FOR JOEY'S

When you exit Joey's garage, you'll notice that there are now two blue blips on the radar—Luigi's "L" and now Joey's "J." That means you've got two people you can visit to get work. For Joey's jobs, step into the Blue Marker outside his garage between the hours of 06:00 and 21:00. (This is military time. These jobs must be done after 6:00AM and before 9:00PM.)

BITCH 'N' DOG FOOD FACTORY

Do you hear that? It's the sound of a phone ringing. This may remind players of how they got jobs in previous GTA games. You can answer the call on the next block to the east to begin jobs for Marty Chonk, the owner of the Bitch 'n' Dog Food plant. However, let's just keep Luigi, then Joey, happy for now.

LUIGI 4: PUMP ACTION PIMP

PAYOFF: $4000

JOB DESCRIPTION: Knock off Diablo pimp invading Luigi's backyard with a firearm from AmmuNation.

Go and take care of things for me.

Leave the Sex Club 7's back alley and head to the Green Gun icon on the radar in the St. Mark's area. Enter AmmuNation and notice the two "out of stock" gun selections they have. The owner of the shop says there's a nine in the yard behind the shop.

AMMUNATION

Keep this place in mind after this job so you can return to buy weapons instead of risking the Wanted Level when stealing them from people. Avoid shooting a gun inside the shop because the owner has his own shotgun!

Pick up the piece back there and practice your shooting skills (see *Chapter 1: Game Basics*). Be aware that shooting in the city will attract cops. The gun you found has only 12 shots, so don't practice away all your rounds.

Jump into a car and head toward the red blip on the radar. This is the pimp's car.

Try to catch the car while it's stopped at a light or in traffic. If you don't get this chance, then swerve your vehicle into the Diablo Stallion's path to force a stop. These thugs are very evasive and will even attack you when provoked—with or without their car! Exit your vehicle and enter the driver's side of the Diablo car to throw the driver to the ground.

STALLION DAMAGE

The pimp will not exit the car until damage is done to the Diablo Stallion.

Quickly exit the vehicle, then select your gun, target with the R1 button, and shoot the driver until he doesn't get up. Be careful, he's got an Uzi!

28

Enter the Diablo Stallion once more. You'll be safe with the pimp in the car as long as he stays put. Drive to a remote area without any cops, then enter the passenger side to eject the pimp. Shoot him before he has a chance to get up and put him down for good.

HENCE, THE PUMP ACTION

The pimp has a pump action shotgun, so move continuously while you have him locked in your sights.

PERSISTENT DRIVER

This is very cool. If you don't knock off the driver and take off with the pimp, the driver will steal a car and give chase. You must take out the driver, as well as the pimp, to complete the mission, so track him down if he doesn't find you. Look for the green blip on the radar.

ALTERNATIVE STRATEGY

Just keep banging their car up with yours until either one is about to explode, then flee the scene before the exploding car takes them both out!

GUN STOCKED

Upon completing this mission, a message appears in the top-left corner of the screen informing you that you may now purchase the pistol at the AmmuNation Gun Shop for 250 bucks.

LUIGI 5: THE FUZZ BALL

TIME LIMIT: 5 MINUTES
PAYOFF: $4000
JOB DESCRIPTION: Get Luigi's girls to the Policemen's Ball before the cops drink away their green.

There are eight girls to pick up and deliver to the old school where the Policeman's Ball is being held. You need to deliver only four of them to pass this mission, but you get 500 dollars for each girl that makes it to the ball. The trick to this mission is having the right vehicle. Most vehicles with a decent back seat will fit three people—vans, cabs, sedans, or police cars.

BUS STATION

If you thought about bringing a bus (Coach) from the Trenton bus station to Luigi's before you started the mission, you're not alone. The bus will fit everyone that needs to be picked up, but you may run out of time because it's so slow.

Fill your vehicle with three girls, then drop them off at the ball and quickly go back for more.

Protect the Girls!

POLICE REPORT

☐ PRIMARY ☐ SUPP   PAGE _____

You will fail the mission if just one of the girls gets run over.

Head south from Luigi's around the next block (Chinatown) to pick up the closest girl. Continue due south for the next girl by the traffic-blocking posts.

Next, head toward the pink blip on the radar (the Policeman's Ball), then pass it as you head south to Trenton to get the third girl. Take all three ladies to the ball and stop in the Blue Marker to let them out. Handbrake power slide into the Marker so that you are facing away from the building for a quicker getaway.

PARKED POLICE CARS

If your vehicle has suffered major damage, then quickly hop into one of the cruisers in the old school's lot for a new ride.

On your next trip, return to Trenton and pick up the girl standing in front of the Portland Docks billboard. Head north and take the next right to get the "girl on the corner" in St. Mark's, then turn around and get back on Portland Docks street and drive north. Take the first right again and you'll see the last girl you can fit in the car. Bring the three of them to the ball. There are two remaining girls—one's in Harwood near the car crusher and the other is on the overpass south of there.

COMPLETELY DIFFERENT

You can pick up the girls in any order you want, but their locations cause you to find quicker routes to pick them up. Following a route that's the complete opposite order from the way mentioned in this section is a good alternative.

JOEY LEONE

JOEY 1: MIKE "LIPS" LAST LUNCH

TIME LIMIT: 5 MINUTES
PAYOFF: $10,000
JOB DESCRIPTION: Steal "Lips" Forelli's car at the St. Mark's Bistro, take it to 8-Ball's bomb shop in Harwood to have it fitted with the bomb, then return and park the car where you found it.

Fast Car

Find a fast and durable car before entering Joey's Garage for a head start on the countdown that starts as soon as you exit the garage.

The Clock is Ticking!

POLICE REPORT
☐ PRIMARY ☐ SUPP   PAGE _____

If you don't have everything set up in five minutes, Lips will be done eating and you'll fail the mission.

Speed to the edge of St. Mark's district and pull into the parking lot of Marco's Bistro (notice the faded green painted sign on the wall of the building next door). Park next to the black car with the Blue Arrow over it. If you reach this point within a minute, you're doing great.

Enter the black car (Idaho) and carefully drive it to 8-Ball's for a bomb. There is enough time to go to Pay 'n' Spray if necessary, but avoid even scratching the car to save the $1000 it'll cost you to have it fixed. Lips will notice even the slightest scratch, so be very careful.

8-Ball's place shows up on the radar as a black 8-Ball with a red ring around it. Once you arrive, your worst nightmare awaits. 8-Ball's driveway looks like the trenches of WWII. Gently pull the car into the garage at the end of the dirt path. If you've still got a couple of minutes on the clock when you leave 8-Ball's, then you're doing fine.

Drive Carefully!

POLICE REPORT
☐ PRIMARY ☐ SUPP   PAGE _____

This kind of damage definitely necessitates a trip to Pay 'n' Spray—and you can kiss $1000 goodbye!

Park the car back into the same spot at the Bistro (in the Blue Marker). Pull straight in and make sure you leave it exactly as you found it.

INDUSTRIAL | PORTLAND |

JOEY 1: MIKE "LIPS" LAST LUNCH

When it's all good, press the Circle button to activate the bomb. The next time the engine is started, the bomb will explode. Get out of the car and don't touch the controller until you automatically close the car door! If you dart off too quickly, you'll leave the door open and Lips will definitely know something's up.

It's Da Bomb!

POLICE REPORT
☐ PRIMARY ☐ SUPP PAGE _____

If the door is open and the bomb is set, don't try to re-enter the car to close the door.

If all goes well, Lips will exit the Bistro and start up the car—and Boom! There goes his lunch.

JOEY 2: FAREWELL "CHUNKY" LEE CHONG

PAYOFF: $10,000
JOB DESCRIPTION: Take out "Chunky" Lee Chong in Chinatown for Joey.

After receiving the details of your new job for Joey, head to AmmuNation for a piece. If you already have a gun, then fuhgetaboudit!

Head to the green blip on the radar (Chunky in his stand) in the market area of Chinatown—this area is blocked off to cars.

Pull out your piece and use the target button to pick out the Triad gang members—they're the ones with the blue coveralls wielding bats and guns. Use the L2 and R2 Buttons to select the Triads out of the crowd. You don't have the time to waste on civilian incidents and you can't spare your ammo on them right now anyway.

Two guys with bats and another one with a gun show up. Use your selective aim to take the guy with the gun out first, then dispatch the Triads with bats. You'll probably alert the cops, so don't stand around too long. Get a car and chase after Chong, who's on his way in a getaway car.

If you get too far away from Chunky Lee's car, he'll get away and you'll lose the mission. Stay close and ram his vehicle. Get him jammed where his car won't move and then pull him out of the vehicle. Get out and chase Chunky as he runs away. Beat'm, shoot'm, and do whatever it takes to delete him.

JOEY 3: VAN HEIST

TERMS: DON'T LET SECURICAR GET AWAY!
PAYOFF: $20,000
JOB DESCRIPTION: Get a car and ram the payroll van in Chinatown until the security guard bails, then take the van to the warehouse at the Portland Docks.

As you exit Joey's Garage, notice the blue Damage Meter under the Wanted Level. This is not your damage; it's the Securicar's. Jump into your car and track down the Securicar—look for the red blip on the radar.

When you find the Securicar, ram into it repeatedly and watch the Damage Meter. Your vehicle will most likely be weaker so you'll eventually have to bail out of it. Slow the Securicar down with your car and quickly find another to continue the chase.

Once the Damage Meter is maxed, the driver will run off. Seize the Securicar and drive it to the lock up at the Portland Docks (follow the pink blip on the radar). Pull into the open storage room, then get out and exit the room. Joey's boys will crack it open for the loot. Collect a whopping $20,000!

EL BURRO
After finishing this van heist for Joey, El Burro will page you. He's heard about you and wants to race. You can go now, but let's deal with Joey's jobs first.

JOEY 4: CIPRIANI'S CHAUFFEUR

PAYOFF: $3000
JOB DESCRIPTION: Take Toni to Mamma Cipriani's restaurant in St. Mark's.

As you pull out of the garage in the new shiny Mafia Car, Toni asks you to take him to the laundry in Chinatown first. He says he has business to take care of and he's not talking about a load of whites. He says the washer woman isn't payin' protection money anymore.

Head to Chinatown, following the blip on the radar. When you stop in the Blue Marker outside Mr. Wong's Laundrette, Toni gets out of the car, enters the laundry, then quickly runs back out and into the car. It's a Triad ambush! Drive quickly into St. Mark's and into the small parking lot with the Blue Marker—this is the Cipriani Restaurant. You must make sure that the cops are off your tail, so lose the Wanted Level if you have one.

Afterward, Cipriani laughs at the thought of the Triads thinking that they can mess with him. He invites you to come over later so you can take part in the revenge plot.

THE UZI'S IN STOCK

Upon completion of this level, you'll receive a page from AmmuNation Gun Shop informing you that you can now purchase an Uzi! However, you can get one for free on the next block to the south of Toni's. Just follow the sloped alley up to the middle concrete enclosed yard.

JOEY 5: DEAD SKUNK IN THE TRUNK

PAYOFF: $10,000
JOB DESCRIPTION: Take the car stuffed with a stiff at the café near Callahan Point to the crusher in Harwood.

Jump into your stolen vehicle and follow the red blip on the radar to Greasy Joe's Diner in Callahan Point. The Blue Arrow points to the car you need to pick up—it's parked right in front of the diner. As you enter the Manana, you discover the Forelli brothers have planned a little ambush. Their car is parked in the same lot and they're out for blood!

Take off quickly and try to evade the pursuing Forelli's, all the while keeping in the general direction of the car crusher (denoted by the pink blip the radar).

Once you've lost the Forelli car, park the Manana in the Blue Marker before the crusher and exit the vehicle. Unless you're certain that the Forelli's died in a wreck during their pursuit, then don't stand around watching the crusher too long. They may still be hunting you down and will eventually find you.

Listen for gunfire because the Forelli thugs could have exited their vehicle. Take out any enemy that threatens your life. You can enter the van (Pony) in the junkyard and run them over or just handle them in a shootout. Killing the Forelli is not a requirement for collecting the $10,000 reward. When the car is crushed, you'll receive your payment.

34

JOEY 6: THE GETAWAY

PAYOFF: $30,000

JOB DESCRIPTION: Take a car to the safehouse in St. Mark's to pick up a few of Joey's friends who are hitting a bank.

Find a very fast car that seats four (a four-door). The Mafia Car will do nicely. Follow the pink blip to the driveway in St. Mark's, then stop in the Blue Marker and honk the horn to let them know you're waiting. After the three Mafia men enter you vehicle, head for the bank.

Follow the pink blip on the radar to the Blue Marker in front of the bank in Chinatown. The men in black will go in, rob the bank, and come out quickly. When you hear the alarm sound, hit the gas and get out of there! The cops are going to be all over you like stink on a skunk. You'll be given a Wanted Level of 3.

As you run from the cops, find the Police Bribe (star icons) in their usual places to reduce your Wanted Level or just go to the Pay 'n' Spray to take care of all three Wanted Level stars. Follow the pink blip back to St. Mark's and the Blue Marker in the driveway where you originally picked the men up. You won't feel so bad about paying $1000 for a paint job after collecting your $30,000 reward for completing the mission!

industrial portland

TONI CIPRIANI

TONI 1: TAKING OUT THE LAUNDRY

PAYOFF: $20,000

JOB DESCRIPTION: Destroy all of Mr Wong's laundry vans and mangle anyone who gets in the way.

Before leaving Toni with his mom, he tells you that 8-Ball has what you need to get the job done. Actually, you don't need to pick up the grenades from 8-Ball—they're good to have, but not necessary.

There are four vans running around town; each is appears as a red blip on the radar. The object is to destroy the vans. You don't need to throw grenades at them to do this. There are many ways to get rid of a vehicle, as you already know. Be creative—you can shoot them, throw the drivers out, and then enter the vans.

Being at the steering wheel opens up an endless number of opportunities. Drive them to the Portland Beach, park them at the edge of the sea, and let them roll in and sink under the water. Push them off a pier using another vehicle. Take them to the crusher. Get them fitted with bombs at 8-Ball's. Roll them, ram them—whatever it takes to destroy all four of them. Do this and Toni pays you $20,000. Not bad, not bad at all! Except that now you'll have to do your own laundry.

TONI 2: THE PICK-UP

PAYOFF: $10,000

JOB DESCRIPTION: Collect the recently reinstated protection payment from the laundry, prepared for another Triad ambush.

Follow the light blue blip on the radar to Mr Wong's laundry, then drive around to the back loading docks through the connecting alleyways. You'll see the briefcase with the Blue Arrow over it. Park close to the money with your vehicle directly facing an exit from the alleyway before you get out.

Toni was right... it's going to get ugly. As soon as you jump out of the car and grab the briefcase, a cinematic will show a mess of Triads coming from all three exits!

36

Quickly jump into the car and run over anyone in your path. Before entering the street, press L2+R2 for the rearview visual, then throw the car into reverse to run over anyone you missed. Keep going until you've hit the opposite street. Enter another time and head down the third alley just to make sure you got them all. The alley is so narrow that there's nowhere for them to run!

The alleyway facing the loading doors happens to be blocked by the last Triad member who's commandeered a large Belly-Up truck. Shoot him or take his truck and run him over.

Take the money back to Toni and he'll give you your cut... 10,000 big ones!

TONI 3: SALVATORE CALLED A MEETING

PAYOFF: $15,000

JOB DESCRIPTION: When you arrive at Cipriani's Restaurant, you'll find a letter but no Toni. The letter reads: Don Salvatore has called a meeting. I need you to collect the limo and his boy, Joey, from the garage. Then get Luigi from his club, come back and pick me up, then we'll all drive over to the boss's place together. Those Triads, they don't know when to stop. They want a war. They got a war.

Head to Joey's garage in Trenton (the pink blip on the radar) and step into the Blue Marker. Inside, you'll find yourself behind the wheel of a limo and Joey will hop in the back.

The "Stretch" limo is no sports car, but what a looker! It's very sluggish and will take a while to climb hills, so try to avoid slowing down before inclines.

Follow the next blip to Luigi's club in the Red Light District and park in the Blue Marker. Honk the horn and Luigi will join Joey in the backseat.

Finally, head to St. Mark's to pick up Toni. Before you sound the horn, make sure the limo is facing toward the alley across the street where the Toyz van is parked.

As soon as Toni hops in, multiple Belly-Up trucks will come from either direction on the main road and slam into the limo until it is destroyed! If any of the bosses die, the mission will end unsuccessfully. The alley is the only escape route—no trucks will be come from that direction.

If you step on the gas as soon as control returns to you following the cinematic, you'll have time to dart into the alley and begin your escape route to Salvatore's house in Portland Beach (the blip on the radar).

Make a few rights as you exit the alley with the Toyz van and continue to follow the blip. When you reach Salvatore's driveway, you'll see two Belly-Up trucks blocking the way.

Swing around and come at them from the south. There's a space between the back of the first truck and the edge of the apartment building. Squeeze through here to make the driveway. You'll run over a guarding Triad in the process.

When you pull up to Salvatore's mansion, the garage door will open, allowing you to park the limo inside and escape the madness. The Don is pleased with your work and you collect $15,000!

THE BOYS ARE BUSY

After meeting Salvatore Leone, the bosses you brought here will not offer any work until you take care of the Don's first request. Head toward the big "S" on the radar to pick up the first Salvatore Leone job.

salvatore Leone
salvatore 1: CHaPerone

PAYOFF: $10,000
JOB DESCRIPTION: Drive the Don's girl, Maria, to a party in the Atlantic Quays, then bring her home without any trouble.

Drive the limo to the waterfront in Chinatown near the El Train Station. Move into the Blue Marker and Maria will exit the limo to talk to Chico about a party. When she returns, head to the Atlantic Quays where you'll find a party heating up in a warehouse.

Similar to the last limo mission, the positioning of the vehicle when you park is key. Pull into the parking lot, then turn around so that the nose of the limo is facing the main street and the back is facing the sea. When you stop in the Blue Marker, Maria will get out and enter the party in the warehouse. Hang tight, she won't be long. The cops are tipped off on the party and initiate a raid on the rave!

Luckily, Salvatore has a police scanner installed in the limo and you're ready for a quick getaway. As soon as Maria gets in the car, speed forward through the crowd of cops and wiseguys.

Take her back home as quickly as possible. You'll have a Wanted Level 2 and tons of cops looking for you! Park the car in Salvatore's garage again to finish the job. The Don pays pretty well... $10,000!

mafia cars
You won't have to look long for a nice ride when you're at the Don's house. Those two Mafia cars in the driveway are yours for the taking!

Toni 4: Triads and Tribulations

PAYOFF: $30,000
JOB DESCRIPTION: Take a few of Toni's boys down to the fish market in Chinatown and whack the Triad Warlords, along with any of their soldiers that get in the way.

Two men in black follow you as you leave Toni's patio. They will continue to follow your every move—in and out of vehicles, in and out of battle—until you or they die. Don't worry—they're on your side.

industrial PORTLANd

State of Emergency!

POLICE REPORT

☐ PRIMARY ☐ SUPP PAGE _____

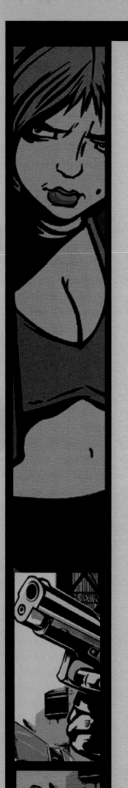

There's a war on the streets! Three outfits are battling amongst themselves and you're caught in the middle. Try not to huff in on foot too much. Drive as often as possible to avoid intentional fire and crossfire attacks.

Jump into a car and wait to take off until both men have entered the vehicle. Head to any one of the three green blips on the screen. Each one will lead you to a Triad Warlord and his surrounding soldiers.

CHiNATOWN WARLORDS

One of the Chinatown Warlords is located in the same parking lot as the stairs that lead up to the Chinatown El Train station. Using your car as a weapon is the safest way to eliminate this Warlord. His many soldiers make this area very unsafe. Cops will more than likely be alerted and thrown into the mix, too.

The Warlord is the guy with a Blue Arrow over his head. Take him out and don't worry about the rest of the gang unless you want to augment your arsenal with a few more weapons by participating in the street wars.

BeLLY-UP

A Belly-Up truck is parked in the lot where this battle takes place. Before you leave this area, take the truck or one of the many just like it—you'll need it when you leave Chinatown.

There is one more Warlord in Chinatown and he's hanging out in the fish market area (the area blocked off to vehicles). It's going to be a gun battle. Run through the market area, then press the R1 button when you approach the Warlord, standing alone in the middle of the market walkway. This will allow you to auto-track him as you shoot him up.

CALLAHAN POINT WARLORD

In a Belly-Up truck, follow the green blip on the radar. Pull onto the dirt road off of the main street and approach the Turtle Head Fishing Co. warehouse's electric gate. The gate will open only for the Belly-Up truck that you've commandeered. Drive around the building, running over soldiers until you can squash the guy with the Blue Arrow looming over his head. Once you've taken out the Warlord and most of his soldiers, jump out of the truck and pick up the special Package in the back of the building.

40

TONI 5: BLOW FISH
PAYOFF: $30,000
JOB DESCRIPTION: Carefully drive the Trashmaster rigged with a bomb to the fish factory and park it between the gas canisters. Set the bomb, then get the hell out of there!

The red blip on the radar will direct you to 8-Ball's. Once you arrive, head to the left of his garage to the train tracks to find the giant Trashmaster. Jump into the driver's seat and get a feel for the handling—quickly. You have less than two-and-a-half minutes to deliver the bomb to the fish factory!

Drive very carefully. You really don't have to worry about your speed, since it's not really possible, but you do have to be very good at navigating the roads. Don't hit anything. It will sustain small impacts, but it's hard to predict just what might trigger the bomb inside the truck.

Take It Easy!

POLICE REPORT
☐ PRIMARY ☐ SUPP PAGE _____

Drive this Trashmaster the way you would if your mother was in the passenger seat next to you. She may not be proud of your job (Trashmaster or crook) but consider the wheels you can afford.

Follow the pink blip on the radar all the way to Callahan Point, into the Turtle Head Fish Factory's electric gate. Go to the opposite side of the building to find the Blue Marker. Press the Circle button to activate the bomb, then exit the Trashmaster and head for cover!

SALVATORE 2: CUTTING THE GRASS
PAYOFF: $15,000
JOB DESCRIPTION: Follow Curly Bob's taxi home from his bartending job at Luigi's club. If he's been rattin' on Salvatore, kill him.

Take one of Salvatore's Mafia Cars and head over to Luigi's Sex Club 7 in the Red Light District. Park north of the entrance and watch the taxi on the corner in front of the club. Curly will come out of the alley and enter the cab.

A Spookometer will appear below your Wanted Level. The object is NOT to spook Curly. Don't let him know he's being followed. Stay several car lengths behind him to avoid registering anything on the Spookometer, but stay close enough to keep him in sight. The cab does not appear on the radar, but a Blue Arrow identifies it on screen.

Follow Curly to the Portland Docks. A cinematic will show him leave the cab and talk with Catalina and Miguel. Turns out Curly's spilling the beans afterall. He tells the Colombians that the Leones are in a war on two fronts. They've got a turf battle with the Triads and are stirring up bad blood with the Forelli family—and Salvatore is suspecting everything and everyone.

When control returns to you, you get the "go" to whack Curly for talking. Locate him on the radar (the green blip). Run over him with the car or shoot him Mafia style. Be careful, though—he's toting a shotgun. Curly Bob is near the trailer offices in front of the large warehouse. Jump out of the car and find the Adrenaline power-up surrounded by the trailers, then smack him with super human strength! When the deed is done, you collect the dough... $15,000 to be exact.

Pager message

If you haven't already taken care of the Triads and Tribulations job for Toni, then he'll page you when you complete this job for Salvatore. He says he wants you to take care of the Triad Warlords. This must be done to receive Salvatore's next job.

Salvatore 3: Bomb Da Base

PAYOFF: $100,000
JOB DESCRIPTION: Destroy the floating SPANK factory with explosives from 8-Ball.

Take a Mafia Car over to 8-Ball's (the green "8" on the radar). When you arrive at your buddy's auto yard, head around to the side of the building adjacent to his bomb-fitting facility to find a Blue Marker. Step into it. One of two things will happen, he'll either help you or he won't. It will take $50,000's worth of explosives to sink the ship—and this comes out of YOUR pocket!

Bomb Da Base (Parts 1 & 2)

Part 1 of Bomb da Base ends as you leave Salvatore's house. Part 2 begins when you enter the Blue Marker at 8-Ball's auto yard with enough money to give to purchase the expensive explosives.

8-Ball may be your pal and all, but he won't take an IOU, so you'll have to come up with the money if you don't already have it. If you've been following along with the guide and have completed all the missions up until now, you'll either have the money or come real close, depending on how many times you've lost money from going to the hospital, getting Busted, or paying to have your cars painted. Take any of the little missions like Marty Chonks, the Toyz vans, or the Patriot Playground to make up the difference. You could even try to find more of the Hidden Packages, attempt some jumps and stunts, or take some Taxi jobs... the list goes on and on. There are plenty of ways to make trouble and earn some cash.

When you've got the dough, 8-Ball hands you a sniper rifle. Enter the nearest vehicle (there's usually a van in front of the auto yard and the Banshee in the AUTOS dealership is not far). Allow 8-Ball to enter the vehicle before taking off without him. If you smash or have to leave your vehicle, 8-Ball will follow you.

Follow the pink blip to Portland Harbor and enter the Blue Marker near the docks. 8-Ball instructs you to find a good vantage point to shoot while he sets the explosives.

As 8-Ball heads for the colorful storage containers, you should take the car toward the Les Cargo ship. There's a set of stairs leading to the roof on the corner of the building facing the ship. Climb to the first landing for a great view of all the Colombian guards on and off the ship.

SNiPER RiFLE CONTROLS
Press and hold R1 button to target; Square button = zoom in; X button = zoom out; Circle button = fire. Aim true... you have 30 rounds of ammo.

Since 8-Ball will start up the ramp to the ship as the first shot is fired, it's best to take out the two guards watching the ramp first. In fact, the whole mission can be accomplished by starting with the left-most guy (next to the ramp), then taking out the guy on the right, and then continuing to dispatch the guards from left to right aboard the ship.

Aim for the noggin to see the killer head shot animation, although a hit anywhere on the body of these Colombians will put them down for good. When you shoot the first guy (left of the ramp), the second (right of the ramp) will run for cover behind the Colombian car. His entire upper body will still be visible though and you can get a good shot from your position.

Quickly clear all 10 guards on the ship before 8-Ball makes it up there or else they'll start shooting at him as he approaches. To make it easy on you, take aim at the head of the first guy near the ramp onboard, take the shot, and then avoid adjusting the up and down aiming until you have to. Just use the left and right aiming to focus your shot at the rest of the Colombians. You will need to raise the scope only if you want to hit the guy standing on the crates in the head and not in the legs, but this is not necessary. A leg shot will do.

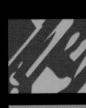

When done correctly, 8-Ball will run into the hull of the ship, plant the explosives, then run back down the ramp just as the ship explodes and sinks. You not only earn $100,000 from this job, you'll also have access to the Colombian cars near the sinking ship. These vehicles are pretty tough, but they roll over easily.

SaLVaTore 5: LasT RequesTs

Payoff: $20,000
Job Description: Take a brain-splattered car parked around the block from Luigi's Sex Club 7 to the crusher.

Follow the red blip to the sports car behind Luigi's. When you enter Chinatown and the Red Light District area, you'll receive a page. Pay attention to the message—it will save your life. It's a page from Maria, Salvatore's girl. She says the car is a trap and you should meet her at slip south of Callahan Bridge. You'll now see Maria indicated by a pink dot on the radar.

DON't NeeD a CHeeTaH

If you enter the Cheetah in the alley, you won't have enough time to escape with your limbs attached. The car is rigged with a bomb. Could 8-Ball be involved in this plot to assassinate you?

THE SLiP

Drive into the tunnel near the Callahan Bridge in the Red Light District and you'll emerge at the slip in Callahan Point. Drive into the Blue Marker at the end of the road and a cinematic will show Maria spilling her guts about Salvatore.

DON't fear THe Reefer

You, Maria, and her friend, Asuka, step aboard the Reefer and leave Portland. The boat controls are similar to driving a car except there are no brakes, just reverse. If you've never navigated a boat before, you'll quickly learn that you must give it gas to turn. When you press the Triangle button to stop commanding the Reefer, you won't hop out of the boat automatically. You must do this manually if there isn't a Blue Marker to drive into.

"Sea" THe PacKaGe?

Have a look around just off the shores of Portland. You'll find a Hidden Package on a small island of rocks. You may not be able to get back on the boat (it may float away), but you'll still have your Package if you end up at the hospital,.

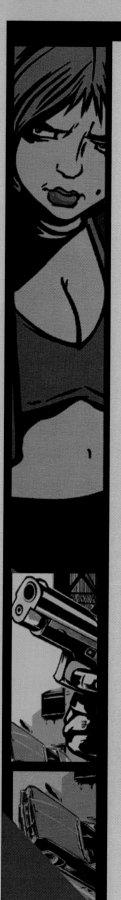

Navigate toward the pink blip on the radar. This is the Blue Marker at the docks in Staunton Island. After being welcomed to Staunton Island, the girls depart. Asuka directs you to a place where you can lie low for a while—your saving Hideout at the edge of Belleville in Staunton Island. When the mission ends, you'll have $20,000 more in your pocket. Take this time to explore and save your progress at your new Hideout.

STAUNTON ISLAND

You now have access to the entire area of Staunton Island. Take this time to get familiar with the roads and the people and the cars. There are lots of nice sports cars and SUVs to be had.

COMMUTING

All the routes between Portland and Staunton Island are now accessible—the Callahan Bridge is fixed, the Subway is open, the underwater tunnel is available, and there are boats at the docks.

INDUSTRIAL DISTRICT EXTRA MISSIONS

The following jobs are not necessary to complete the game, but you'll miss out on a bunch of money and fun if you don't take them.

EL BURRO

EL BURRO 1: TURISMO

PAYOFF: $10,000

JOB DESCRIPTION: After getting El Burro's page, head to Hepburn Heights and follow the blue blip on the radar. Answer the phone and accept El Burro's challenge to a race by the old school hall.

This is El Burro of the Diablos.

Before entering the automobile you drove to the phone booth, look around for a Diablo Car. They're almost everywhere you look—if you don't jump into the car you drove up in. Take a Diablo Car to the pink blip on the radar, near the Callahan Bridge and the old school hall. Pull into the Blue Marker next to the other Diablo Cars and watch the 3-second countdown.

FIND YOUR OWN RIDE!

You cannot use the three Diablo Cars waiting to race. The doors won't open and they may even shoot at you for trying. You must race against the three Diablo Cars.

As the countdown ends and the tires begin to scream, wait a second and let the three Diablo Cars take off ahead of you. This is a guiltless maneuver for various reasons. First, you'll know where you are going if you follow closely behind the Diablos (the race will take you through various Portland checkpoints). Follow the Diablos for the best route.

Secondly, the Diablos are nuts! In the first few turns, they're all trying to take each other out! Let them, then follow the lead or take your own lead while they recover from some serious twisted metal.

If you're in the lead, watch the radar closely to find the nearest pink blip—this will lead you to the next checkpoint marker.

THE SWITCH

If your car is getting trashed, grab a Mafia Car or something else equally as swift. You don't have to be in a Diablo Car to finish the race successfully.

This is a pretty lengthy race that'll send you around the city a few times on different streets. There are 18 checkpoints, including the red one at the finish line just beyond the old school where you started. The race should take you about two minutes to complete. The reward for a first place finish is $10,000!

46

EL BURRO 2: I SCREAM, YOU SCREAM

PAYOFF: $6000

JOB DESCRIPTION: Pick up the hidden bomb in Harwood, hijack the regular ice-cream van on its route, and lure the Forelli gang to their doom—a warehouse in Atlantic Quay.

First, you need to pick up the briefcase containing the bomb. Follow the blue blip on the radar over the overpass, a block away in Harwood. You'll see the Blue Arrow pointing to the briefcase in a small parking lot. Pick it up and search for the ice cream—follow the red blip on the radar. You should catch up to the van somewhere around St. Mark's. Block the van with your vehicle, then toss out the driver and speed away in your shiny, new "Mr. Whoopee" ice cream truck.

Follow the pink blip on the radar into the Atlantic Quays. Drive over the cones that line the entrance to the warehouse hideout of the ice cream adoring gang. Park the van in the Blue Marker, then press the L1 button and hold it as the melody plays to attract the sugar hungry gang. When the Forelli thugs arrive, exit the vehicle and move far away. Notice that there's a detonator in your hand. Once you reach a safe distance, push the Circle button to activate the bomb. KA-BOOM! $6000 for you. Gather weapons from the carnage.

EL BURRO 3: TRIAL BY FIRE

PAYOFF: $10,000

JOB DESCRIPTION: Pick up the flame-thrower and teach the Triad vandals to fear El Burro's wrath.

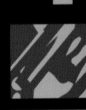

Go to Chinatown, following the gun icon on the radar to an alley where there used to be a Rampage power-up. That power-up is now a flame-thrower. This mission is very similar to a Rampage challenge: you must use a weapon with unlimited ammo to knock off a plethora of people in a certain amount of time. However, this challenge affords you one more minute to dispatch 10 more people.

Take the flame-thrower out to the street and waste 30 Triads in three minutes. Head to the nearest intersection to get the most Triad traffic. The biggest thing to worry about is not burning yourself in the process. Try to keep your distance from the future crispies and don't burn anyone beside you—the fire will spit back in your face and cause you damage.

industrial
: portland :

If you're having trouble finding 30 Triads, go a block south to the basketball court in the park. Triads like basketball so you'll easily meet the toast quota here! When it's all said and well done, you'll earn $10,000! Collect the weapons and head to the hospital if you need to recover from any burns.

EL BURRO 4: BIG 'N' VEINY

PAYOFF: $20,000
JOB DESCRIPTION: After getting the scoop in the phone booth, take the van and collect the trail of adult magazines, then deliver them to XXX Mags in the Red Light District.

El Burro's collection van is parked right outside the Hepburn Heights parking lot. Enter the Rumpo van and drive north through the bundles of magazines. You must follow this trail of magazines to find his stolen van. That's not the worst of it, though. You begin with only 20 seconds to finish the course! Every magazine bundle you drive through gives you an additional second... yeah, only one second. Stay on target and don't stray too far off the trail.

XXX MAGS
The pickups are not indicated on the radar as the checkpoints were during the Diablo Car race. This means you must keep an eye on the road. You DO NOT have to pick up all the magazines to accomplish this mission.

In the first stretch of the course all the turns are to the left (just in case you are looking for the magazine bundles when they disappear in the intersections). You'll head past Salvatore's home on your way to Chinatown from St. Mark's. Traffic will get a little heavier and the cars will try to spin you around as they zoom through intersections.

In Chinatown there is also a series of left turns until you near the fish market and the bank. At that point, you'll start with the right turns.

As you approach the Red Light District, the trail suddenly cuts to the south toward the Callahan Bridge.

Continue to follow the trail of porn through Callahan Point, then turn right into the Atlantic Quays—where the ice cream truck was detonated. Don't miss this detour; you'll need the bonus seconds.

The trail picks up again in Trenton. At the next intersection, when you can't see the next bundle, turn right to pick up the trail again. Swerve into the Portland Docks and follow the trail left through an alleyway. After a few more pickups, you'll see the stolen van with a Blue Arrow over it.

The thief is standing at the back of the van. Sandwich him between the two vehicles to squish him, then return the stolen goods to the back of XXX Magazines in the Red Light District (follow the pink blip on the radar).

correct van

Make sure you take the van you're driving to XXX Magazines. You've been collecting all the mags in your van, so the El Burro's stolen van is empty.

When you drive into the Blue Marker behind the store, a cinematic will show the men of Liberty City very satisfied by your delivery. You should be excited, too, with your $20,000 reward!

MARTY CHONKS: BITCH 'N' DOG FOOD FACTORY JOBS

A phone is ringing a block east from Joey's Garage (after delivering Misty to Joey in mission, *Luigi 3: Drive Misty for Me*). Pick it up to get jobs from Marty Chonks, the owner of the Bitch 'n' Dog Food plant.

MARTY CHONKS 1: THE CROOK

PAYOFF: $1000

JOB DESCRIPTION: Pick up the bank manager in Marty's Car and bring him back to the Bitch 'n' Dog Food Factory.

Walk up to the gate on caddy-corner from the phone. It will open as you approach it. Head around to the back of the factory and find Marty's car behind a tractor-trailer. Nice wheels, Marty... it's a station wagon!

MARTY'S CARS

Marty always supplies his own cars for you to use on his jobs, so don't wreck 'em! If you destroy his cars, you'll fail his missions.

Drive the "Perennial" (and hope it lives up to the name) toward the green blip on the radar. This will take you to the Bank Manager outside his place of work in Chinatown. Simply drive him back to the Dog Food Factory, then enter the Blue Marker and stop. The banker gets out of the car, enters the factory, and gets whacked! The job's not over yet—take the car to the crusher to get rid of the evidence!

Follow the pink blip on the radar to the Harwood Junkyard, avoiding pedestrians to keep the fuzz off you. Drive to the back of the junkyard and enter the Blue Marker near the crusher. Stop the car in the marker and get out. Watch as the car gets lifted and squished! You now have $1000 more than you did a moment ago. Return to Marty's for more work (the pink blip on the radar).

CRUSHER 24/7:

This crusher is operable at all times, even though the Blue Marker will not appear here again! Using the crusher is a great way to get rid of a vehicle. Just park the car under the magnet and clear out!

50

marty chonks 2: the thieves

PAYOFF: $3000

JOB DESCRIPTION: Use Marty's car to pick up the insurance fraud thieves in the Red Light District, then bring them back to Marty at the Dog Food Factory.

Get into Marty's Sentinel, found behind the tractor-trailer inside the gates of the Bitch 'n' Dog Food Factory. Follow the green blip on the radar to the Red Light District where you'll see the two thieves standing outside a red painted café. Pick them up and take them back to Marty's inside the gates of the Dog Food Factory. Drive into the Blue Marker and stop. The two crooks will enter the factory to see Marty. As before, when dealing with paranoid Marty, he wants you to respray the car, then ditch it.

Take the car to the Pay 'n' Spray (the orange blip on your radar) and have it repainted. This time you're going to have to pay for the service! Dump the car by the road bridge in Chinatown.

car trouble?

If you ever get a car that's key to the mission stuck in odd terrain or can't get the tires to grip, exit the vehicle, find another one, and gently push the key vehicle out of the hazard. Re-enter the key vehicle and continue the mission.

Follow the pink blip to Chinatown and drive into the park, then stop in the Blue Marker near the bridge. You just netted $2000 (after deducting $1000 from your profits to paint the car). Oh, well… that's the cost of doing business in this shady line of work.

marty chonks 3: the wife

PAYOFF: $2000

JOB DESCRIPTION: Use Marty's car to pick up his wife from Classic Nails, then bring her back to the factory.

This time Marty has an Esperanto waiting for you behind the factory. Exit the parking lot through the gate once again and head for Classic Nails in the Red Light District (the green blip on the radar). Take great care while driving this car and make sure that you don't hurt Mrs. Chonks either—her husband will do that himself. Follow the pink blip on the radar back to the Dog Food Factory and deliver the Missus to Marty.

After the dirty deed has been done dirt cheap, dump the car in the sea. There isn't blip on the map this time to direct you to the watery grave, but you can't miss it.

For fun, head to the Portland Docks, then drive to the back to the actual docks. Pull up onto the freighter, "Les Cargo," using the ramp from the docks and turn to the left once onboard. Point the nose of the car toward the edge of the ship, facing the dock where there are no railings.

Get out of the car, run down the ramp, and get into the truck (Yankee) parked dead ahead against the colorful cargo containers. Drive the truck up the ramp of the ship and, from behind Marty's car, push the vehicle into the sea. Splash, splash, give me the cash! Cha-ching! $2000 for passing the mission.

MARTY CHONKS 4: HER LOVER

PAYOFF: $4000
JOB DESCRIPTION: Take Marty's latest car to pick up his late wife's lover, Carlos, and bring him back to the factory.

Take the Stallion from the Dog Factory parking lot and head to the green blip on the radar. Stop at the apartment building in Chinatown where you'll find Carlos waiting for you—the guy with a Blue Arrow over his head!

Take the lover boy back to Marty's factory. When you pull into the gates, you'll finally see Marty, just standing there, waiting for his wife's fling. Stop into the Blue Marker. Carlos will exit the vehicle and take out Marty with a shotgun! Oops! This ends the Marty Chonks jobs. But hey, you made some cash.

52

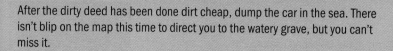

RC TOYZ

RC TOYZ: Mafia Massacre

There's a light blue van with a painted white panel in St. Mark's alley, across the street from Cipriani's Restaurant. Hop in begin a little Toyz Challenge. You must control little RC race cars one at a time into the surrounding streets to destroy Mafia Cars. Press ● to detonate the RC cars next to or under the Mafia Cars. You'll find that controlling these tiny assassins is no different than any other vehicle. When one explodes, the next will immediately launch from the Toyz van for another go. Destroy as many Mafia Cars you can in two minutes. You get $1000 for each successful hit.

RC TOYZ: Diablo Destruction

PAYOFF: $1,000 FOR EACH GANG CAR DESTROYED
JOB DESCRIPTION: The RC Toyz Van, Diablo Destruction, is around the corner from the Hepburn Heights El Train Station. As with any other RC Toyz mission, you have two minutes to blow up as many Diablo Gang Cars (Diablo Stallions) as possible. Press the Circle button to detonate the toy, or ram into the tires of the gang cars.

"diablo destruction"
You have 2 minutes to blow up as many Diablo Gang Cars as possible!

Leave the parking lot by the stairs that lead up to the El Train. The RC car is already pointing in the correct direction each time it reappears after an explosion. Stick to the surrounding block as you look for Diablo Stallions—they will appear. You receive $1,000 for each Diablo Gang Car you annihilate.

4X4

Patriot Playground

Jump into the Hum-V and begin the Patriot Playground challenge at the "Supa Save!" Grocery store in Portland View. You have five minutes to collect 15 checkpoints, which you may gather in any order. A quick cinematic shows you a few locations and what the checkpoints look like—glowing blue markers. The timer will start after you pass through your first checkpoint. Each one will credit you with 20 seconds. Collect all the checkpoints to earn $30,000.

54

3

COMMERCIAL STAUNTON ISLAND

INTRODUCTION

STAUNTON ISLAND HIDEOUT

Your new Hideout location is in Belleville Park (the pink house on the radar). Here, you'll have a garage for saving two cars, as well as an elevator you enter to initiate the save. As with the last Hideout, any special power-ups that you've unlocked by finding the Hidden Packages will appear in this alley. Save after every successful mission.

ASUKA KASEN

ASUKA KASEN 1: SAYONARA SALVATORE

PAYOFF: $25,000

JOB DESCRIPTION: Prove to Asuka that you've broken all ties to your old boss, Salvatore Leone, by knocking off him off on his way home from Luigi's club in Portland.

You have three hours to get to where you want to be in Portland. This time is calculated and displayed in the text on the bottom of the screen as you leave Asuka's. When Salvatore leaves Luigi's club at this time, it won't take him long to reach his mansion. At the club, he'll have the support of two Mafia Sedans (besides his own) full of guards, plus five other guards running around. If you are spotted before Salvatore leaves the club, they'll hunt you down and kill you.

There are plenty of ways to take care of this business. You can use stealth with the sniper rifle, go in with guns blazing, or even chase him off the cliff near his mansion, but the ambush is the most entertaining way to eliminate the Don.

If you don't have the flame-thrower with you after taking this job, then just try the job once to see what happens. If you bite it or Salvatore makes it home safely, then get the flame-thrower in Portland. Grenades and Molotov Cocktails will work almost as well.

FLAME-THROWER IN PORTLAND

Go to the Hepburn Heights El Train Station and walk along the center of the tracks, heading north toward Harwood. As soon as you see the Harwood label appear in the lower-right corner of the screen, begin looking to the left (west) for the roof of the Head Radio Station. You can jump from the tracks down onto the rooftop and, better yet, you can aim for the platform with the flame-thrower on it. If you haven't yet picked up the special Package located on the other end of this roof, then do so now.

FROM ASUKA'S TO THE CALLAHAN BRIDGE

This is the hardest part of the mission. It's tough to make it to Portland in three hours if you can't find the bridge—has anyone seen the bridge?! Follow the directions on this map for the quickest route.

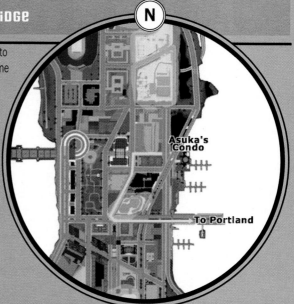

If Salvatore enters his garage, then you fail the mission. Since you know where he's going to be and when, drive to Salvatore's mansion in Portland Beach and park his two Mafia Sedans in front of the garage to the right (the one you parked his limo in). You can even put the car you drove up in, in front of these two—the more explosions the better!

Stand behind the barricading poles where cars are not allowed to drive up the steps of his mansion. When the three Mafia Sedans pull up the drive, start torching them and anyone who escapes the vehicles.

BUGGY BUILT
After you complete this mission, you can head to Misty's between 9:00 and 12:00 to pick up the Buggy that Joey's been working on.

ASUKA KASEN 2: PAPARAZZI PURGE

PAYOFF: $5,000
JOB DESCRIPTION: Get rid of the nosey reporter in the bay near Asuka's house.

Exit Asuka's backyard and head to the second set of docks to the south—not the first set near her house. As you approach the steps, a cutscene shows the reporter's boat out in the bay to the north. Head out to the docks, press the Triangle button when you're near the police boat (just as you would to enter a car). The Circle button will fire the boat's cannons—they occasionally pause for the guns to reload.

Chase the reporter's speedboat toward Portland. Do not allow him to go all the way around Portland and back to these original docks or you'll fail the mission. Closely follow the speedboat and fire the cannons while watching its damage meter. When it's filled, the boat will explode and the mission will end successfully. The speedboat is quicker, so don't fall behind too far or he'll get away. Cut the turns that he takes wide. You know he's going around Portland, so stick with him and keep shooting!

ASUKA KASEN 3: UNDER SURVEILLANCE

PAYOFF: $15,000
JOB DESCRIPTION: Eliminate the Mafia operation around the city for Asuka and you'll be able to pick up some jobs from her brother, Kenji Kasen, when you visit his casino on Staunton Island.

AMMUNATION

You have six-and-a-half minutes to pop nine Mafia men. The good thing about working for Asuka is using her Yakuza Car that's always parked out front! Hop in and speed to any of the green blips on the map. If you don't have the Sniper Rifle, head to the gun icon on the map to find an AmmuNation Gun Shop and stock up on everything you need. The Sniper Rifle is in the back corner for $10,000. It may seem kind of steep, but you need it.

POPPING THE MAFIA

Go to AmmuNation, get the rifle and some grenades, then head to Belleville Park. Try to make this trip in about one minute. Drive to the pond, but not too close—you don't want the two Mafia men to know you're here. They are both on the small island in the middle of the pond. Get out of the car, select the rifle, then take aim and shoot when you're close enough to get a clear shot with the scope fully extended. Take one shot from a spot just east of the cottage, then plant another bullet from the basketball court for another Mafia hit. Get in your car and quickly drive to Bedford Point.

MAFIA VAN-DALIZE

Your next target is a black van in Bedford Point. The third Mafia victim will alert backup. The Sniper Rifle won't work for this task—it's time for the grenades. Pull up behind the van, toss a couple grenades at it, then get back in your car leave. The police and additional backup will begin to swarm you now.

SNIPER HEAVEN

Head east to Torrington and stop at the main entrance to Kenji's Casino. Take the stairs to the top of the building where you'll see the Rockstar helicopter. Head to the western edge and check out the seven Mafia men perched on various balconies across the street. Start at the top and work your way down until you've picked them all off. They will return fire with less-precise Uzis and will be lucky to hit you. It's difficult to score a headshot on the guy on the top floor since you can just barely see his melon, but it is possible—just relax, aim, and shoot. This mission will make you $15,000 richer.

KING COURTNEY

King Courtney of the Yardies pages you after this mission. He wants you to contact him on the payphone (green square on the radar). Stick with Asuka for now—we'll get to King Courtney after the major contacts have been exhausted.

ASUKA KASEN 4: PAYDAY FOR RAY

PAYOFF: $10,000
JOB DESCRIPTION: Meet Asuka's inside man in the LPD to bring him his payment. Go quickly to the pay phone in Torrington and await his instructions.

You have three-and-a-half minutes to find four different phone booths before this shadowing cop will agree to meet with you, so don't waste all that time trying to reach the first phone! Beating the clock is heavily dependent on the car you're driving. With that said, take Asuka's Yakuza Car to the blue blip on the radar, which is a payphone booth in Torrington.

PHONE 1: TORRINGTON

From Asuka's, drive toward the Callahan Bridge, but don't turn left to the bridge. Instead, continue straight through Bedford Point until you see that the blip on the next block to the east. At the phone, powerslide 180 degrees to face the direction you just came, then jump out and get the call.

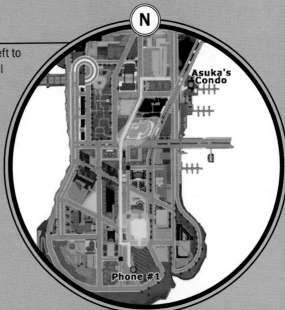

PHONE 2: BELLEVILLE PARK

Jump back in the car and head north down the same street. Take the first left, then right, and left again. This will put on a major road where you'll have plenty of time to react if something jumps out in front of you. Take the second right and you'll see the bay. Stay on this road until you see the phone on the sidewalk to the right, then answer it and jump back in the car.

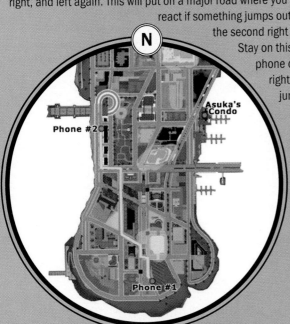

PHONE 3:
LIBERTY CAMPUS

Head north to a freeway support, then merge right and head down the embankment to the road below the overpass. Continue north until you reach the Coliseum with the Rockstar billboards. Turn right, hang a left on the next road in Aspatria, then turn right again into the Liberty Campus. You'll see the phone on the radar. Answer it, then jump back in the car and head west back toward the Coliseum and take a left.

PHONE 4: BELLEVILLE PARK

With the Coliseum on your right, head south until a row of buildings forces you to turn. Turn right, then left at the next road. Go under the overpasses and through a few lights (you will traverse the full length of the park to your left). Turn left at the next intersection. The phone is due east, on the corner in front of a lone building. When you answer the phone, you will be asked to meet Ray in the park and the clock stops. The rest of the mission is just a walk in the park.

60

meeting Ray Machowski

Head to the Belleville Park and meet Ray Machowski in the restrooms. Follow the pink blip on the radar and walk into the Blue Marker. You pay him his money and get an earful from old, bent Ray.

Ray Machowski Jobs

Ray needs some non-union help... that means you. Ray will always be found in the same stinky place—the park restroom. He will appear as a "R" on the radar when you want work. We'll cover his missions after we finish with Asuka and Kenji.

ASUKA KASEN 5: TWO-FACED TANNER

PAYOFF: $20,000
JOB DESCRIPTION: Take care of Tanner, one of Asuka's drivers.

Take Asuka's car and don't worry about the pink blip on the radar just yet. You need to find a big flatbed truck that's almost as strong as a tank! Barrack OLs can be found all over the island. If you have trouble finding one, look on the small base east of the Coliseum. There's an Army Surplus store near the water where you'll find a few parked Army vehicles. The Barracks OL is quite a bit slower than a Yakuza Stinger, but this truck is heavy enough for you to take on an army and the continuous attacks from law enforcement.

The radar will lead you to Kenji's Casino in Torrington. Drive into the Blue Marker and Tanner (Asuka's driver) will come running out of the casino. He gets into an Esperanto and flees. There's a Blue Arrow over his car, a Damage Meter below your Wanted Level, and a red dot on the radar—you know what that means... it's demolition time!

You must chase and ram Tanner's car. As soon as Tanner knows he's being pursued and attacked, he starts to more vigorously evade you and calls for backup. At this point you'll be given an automatic level 5 Wanted Level. That's pretty serious. That means FBI, roadblocks, helicopter... the whole works!

Since you can't keep up with the Esperanto, watch the radar and track Tanner's movements. Try to guess what roads he'll take, then cut through city blocks and try to get a game of chicken going. He seems to always come north along the eastern Shoreside road. This makes pushing him in the bay a wonderful option. The Esperanto is no match for the truck, so the flatbed will bounce him clear into the sky!

KENJI KASEN

KENJI KASEN 1: KANBU BUST-OUT

PAYOFF: $30,000
JOB DESCRIPTION: Break Kanbu out of custody and get him to the dojo at Bedford Point.

STEAL FUZZ WHEELS

As you exit the casino, the first thing you need to do is steal a cop car. Finding a police car is easy, but taking one is a bit more challenging. Pull on the handle of the door or hit the car with yours and get out. Once the cop is out of his squad car, beat him up and drive away in his ride. This gives you a Wanted Level of 1.

8-BALL'S

When you enter the police car, you will be instructed to rig it with a bomb, so take it to 8-Ball's franchise (the 8-Ball icon on your radar). Drive into the garage to plant the explosives.

THE BUST-OUT

Now you must drive into the police compound and park the car next to the cell wall. Follow the pink blip on the radar to the police headquarters' parking lot and drive into the Blue Marker near the wall. Press the Circle button and get out of the cruiser, then run to the parked police truck (Enforcer) on the other side of the lot. Get in this monstrocity when the first police car explodes and blows a piece of the headquarters' wall away. Drive up to the hole in the wall and meet the Yakuza inside if he doesn't run out and get in the truck on his own, then get out of there quickly! You will be given a Wanted Level of 3.

THE ESCAPE

As you drive through the tunnel, you'll find a Police Bribe (Star icon) that will bring your Wanted Level down to 2, which means you'll lose the helicopter pursuit.

Next, switch into a non-law enforcement vehicle and follow the Pay 'n' Spray blip on the radar. Paint the car to totally elude the police, then take the escapee to the Hyaku dojo. Follow the pink blip on the radar to an alley in Bedford Point. Stop on the Blue Marker and Kanbu will enter the dojo. Mission accomplished!

Kenji Kasen 2: Grand Theft Auto

PAYOFF: $25,000
JOB DESCRIPTION: Collect some fine automobiles for Kenji's friend and park them in the garage in Newport.

The garage will not accept anything less than mint condition automobiles. That means a single dent will require a visit to Pay 'n' Spray before making the delivery.

You have six minutes to collect all three cars on the list. The clock is displayed below your Wanted Level. Luckily, the Pay 'n' Spray is next to the drop off garage, so you won't have to go out of your way to fix a boo-boo.

THE RIGHT BLIP

Make sure you follow the right blip! The dark red blips on the radar lead you to the cars while the bright pink blip will lead you to the garage.

THE BEDFORD POINT STINGER

Take the route we've mapped from the casino to the parking lot in Bedford Point, then follow the green line on our map (or the pink dot on the radar) to the garage or Pay 'n' Spray.

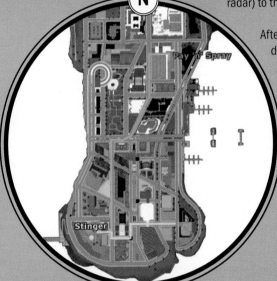

After dropping off the car you'll suddenly realize that you're car-less. Run out to the street and seize a vehicle. There's a Yardie Lobo on the road to the east.

THE ROCKFORD CHEETAH

Head north, past the Pan-Lantic Mask Towers construction site from either road around the garage. Jump the curb of the hospital to access the back parking lot without going all the way around to the entrance. The Cheetah is in the lot. Pull right up to it and head back the same way you came—curb-jump and all. It's quicker to just repair the damaged vehicle than to cautiously navigate on the road. After you make the delivery, steal another car to find the last sports car.

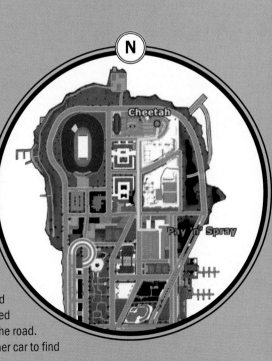

THE ASPATRIA INFERNUS

From the garage, head west to the last red blip on the map in Aspatria. The Infernus is in the Coliseum parking lot. Follow the route on our map—it's the same path you took to reach the parking lot. Deliver all three cars and you'll make 25,000 big ones!

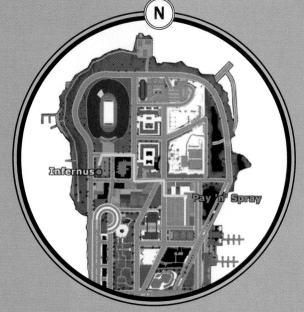

KENJI KASEN 3: DEAL STEAL

PAYOFF: $25,000
JOB DESCRIPTION: Take one of Kenji's men, steal a car, and pay your respects to the Colombians. Leave no one alive!

The Cartel expects a Yardie Posse, so go north to Newport to find the Yardies and take one of their Yardie Lobos.

Once you have possession of a Yardie vehicle, a green blip will appear on the radar. This is the location of the Yakuza member that will help you on your mission. He's on a sidewalk with a Blue Arrow over his head. Stop and pick him up, then head to the hospital in Rockford where the meeting is being held.

Follow the pink blip on the map to the hospital. Drive into the Blue Marker and honk the horn (L3). The Colombians think you're the Yardies coming to meet them and approach the car. You're now instructed to kill every one of them, destroy their vehicles, and then take the briefcase.

As soon as you exit the Yardie Lobo or take off driving, they realize it's actually a Yakuza trap. Swing the car around and run over as many of the Colombians as you can until your vehicle is dangerously close to exploding.

Heart Power-Ups

This meeting takes place at a hospital, so you can heal up here if you're injured.

When you get out of the vehicle and begin a gunfight, your partner will jump out and assist you. A couple of Colombians are near the trucks where you first pulled into the hospital, along with more to the east in the bigger parking lot. The briefcase is near the first set of trucks (the red blip on the map and a Blue Arrow over it).

After first clearing the major threat—the attacking Colombians—take care of the trucks. You'll see Blue Arrows over both trucks that you must destroy.

Friendly Fire

Drive the first Colombian Cruiser over to the bigger parking lot. That way, if the remaining enemies shoot at it, they'll be doing you a favor!

When the shooting's over, park both cars together. Now the explosion from destroying one truck will destroy the other. When the deed is done, take the briefcase back to the casino in Torrington. Follow the pink blip down to the parking lot, then drive into the Blue Marker to make the delivery and collect your $25,000!

KENJI KASEN 4: SHIMA

PAYOFF: $10,000
JOB DESCRIPTION: Pick up some money due to the Yakuza so Kenji can enter it into the casino's accounts. This will involve multiple pick-ups.

Tear out of the casino and follow the blue blip on the radar to a briefcase on a sidewalk in Torrington. Get out of the car, pick it up, and head to the next pick-up location also on the radar as a blue blip.

You'll see another briefcase on a sidewalk in Bedford Point—a lone gunman is guarding this one. If you arrive at this location from the west, you can just smash the gunman into the nearby column. Otherwise, you'll have to swing around while being shot at and run him over.

Hmm... what was up with that? Who was that and why is he getting in the way of Kenji's money? Head to the next briefcase in Belleville Park (pink blip on the radar).

Uncle BJ's has been trashed! The money is gone! The storeowner contests to your suspicions. Some gang attacked and took everything! The storeowner is obviously frustrated since he's paying good money to avoid this kind of trouble.

Your new objective is to find the gang that's responsible for taking the money and make them wish they hadn't, then return the protection money to Kenji.

If you look closely at the radar, you'll see a small blue blip on the border. The gang is distant—in Portland.

Head to Portland and then Hepburn Heights. The blue blip is getting much closer... Ah-ha! The Diablos are behind this! There are quite a few of them in the park that you must dispose of. You can snipe them, run them over, burn them, or bomb them. The choice is yours—just get that briefcase back or face the wrath of Kenji!

Don't stir things up too much—you're a long way from Staunton and you don't need to get busted way over here! Take the briefcase to the back parking lot of Kenji's Casino in Staunton Island and collect $10,000.

KENJI KASEN 5: SMACK DOWN

PAYOFF: $10,000
JOB DESCRIPTION: Run the Yardies into the ground to eliminate their SPANK pushers on Liberty's streets.

As you leave the casino you get the details on your Yardie massacre mission. You must eliminate eight Yardie dealers. Notice the counter located below your Wanted Level.

MURDER BY NUMBERS
The murders need not happen in any particular sequence; the strategy here just discusses them in the order they appear on the list from the Casino.

BEDFORD POINT SPANKERS

The first two Yardies appear as green blips on your radar. Head to Bedford Point where you'll find one of the pushers on the street near the waterfront. Take him down Mafia style, then head toward the next blip. The other pusher in this area is in front of the church of all places! Run him down, that heathen. Head west, remaining in Bedford Point, and you'll see another pusher on the sidewalk closest to the water. Again, turn him into road kill, then keep moving to avoid the cops.

SPANKING IN THE PARK

The pusher in Belleville Park is easily run over on the sidewalk. You'll find another on one of the dirt trails. He's also easy to squish under your tires. There's one more pusher outside of the park to the west. He's on a sidewalk where the buildings have awning supports that may dent your car. Drive on the sidewalk under the awnings and you'll have a clear shot at him.

EVEN IN ASPARTIA—SPANK, SPANK, SPANK!

You'll find another pusher on a sidewalk near the Coliseum. Look out for the college kids— or not. Your next dealing victim is on the corner near the Coliseum parking lot. Just run him over—piece of cake!

When all eight have bit the dust, you'll make another $10,000, but now Kenji's work is all dried up. Oh well, on to the next contact.

RAY MACHOWSKI

RAY MACHOWSKI 1: SILENCE THE SNEAK

PAYOFF: $30,000

JOB DESCRIPTION: Torch McAffrey's place in Newport, then hunt him down to make sure he never squeals again!

Take a car over to the parking lot alley behind the carpark near the Pay 'n' Spray and 8-Ball's. Get the biggest, heaviest, ghetto cruiser you can find and park it right in front of the east alley to block it. You can also take another car, like the van in the garage behind you, and park it there, too. This will really secure the exit. McAffrey will still try to escape through this alley even though there are two other exits that are not blocked. Also, park the car so its hood is along the brick wall and the trunk is facing his building. The driver will always try to push his way out along the brick wall.

Now that the escape route is blocked, look toward the open window you saw in the quick cinematic. Find just the right distance from the apartment window that allows you to lob a grenade or Molotov Cocktail in there with your hardest throw. You don't want to be standing too close to the apartment building should one miss the window and bounce back at you!

Once the place is on fire, McAffrey and his driver flee. A policeman will stay in the garage, so try to ignore him until you complete the ambush. As McAffrey's car turns around and heads toward the blocked alley exit, start lobbing grenades at your parked car and theirs as they try to escape. If this doesn't do the trick, then you'll have to chase McAffrey and try to run him off the road, which is very difficult with a Wanted Level of 2 and all of his police protection.

RAY MACHOWSKI 2: ARMS SHORTAGE

PAYOFF: $10,000

JOB DESCRIPTION: Protect Ray's army buddy's business in Rockford from some Colombian Cartel scum and you'll get some knock-down rates on his weapons.

Follow the pink blip on the radar north of the Coliseum to Phil Cassidy's Army Surplus in Rockford.

car jam

If you jam your car into the path that runs around the building north of the gate, the Cartel will have difficulty sneaking up from another entrance into the gated area.

Approach the gate and it will open. In a cinematic, one-armed Phil will complain about only one of you showing up to help him out of this situation.

He tells you to stock up on the weapons in the area to prepare for the battle. The only thing you need is the rocket launcher on the storage container you passed in the cinematic—did you see it?

As soon as your conversation with Phil ends, return to the building to the north (near the entrance) and head around the northeast side to the path that runs around it. This is the same path that you blocked with your car to prevent unwanted visitors from entering this way.

Jump on the cardboard boxes to the top of the short wall, then walk back toward Phil. Jump from the first storage container to the one with the rocket launcher on it.

There is just enough time to perform this maneuver before the Colombians arrive. Take aim with the R1 button and start blasting their cars as they drive up into the parking lot outside the gate. If any get away, blast the ground near them. If one or two Colombians are hanging around the base of the storage containers, jump down and take them out with a gun or rifle—they're too close to shoot with the rocket launcher.

Don't Kill Phil!   POLICE REPORT

☐ PRIMARY ☐ SUPP   PAGE _____

Phil must live or the mission is over!

Check to see how Phil is doing after the smoke clears. If he's still alive, you'll earn $10,000 and now be able to purchase weapons from him at any time.

PHIL'S DEALS
At Phil's Army Surplus you can purchase the Shotgun for $1500, the M-16 for $5000, and the Rocket Launcher for $25,000. There's also an assortment of army vehicles, but the tank won't open for you now. The only way to get a tank is to steal one when you are at a Wanted Level 6.

RAY MACHOWSKI 3: EVIDENCE DASH

PAYOFF: $10,000
JOB DESCRIPTION: Ram the transport vehicle carrying incriminating photos of Donald Love and collect all the evidence that falls out, then leave it in the car and torch it.

Steal a fast car and find the vehicle that's transporting the evidence (the red blip on the radar). When you spot the Bobcat with the Blue Arrow over it, ram it, then spin around to pick up the package that falls out of the bed. There are five packages in all, and there's no time limit. You will probably have to switch vehicles, depending on the durability of the one you've chosen. You can pick up the packages when you're either in or out of the car. Ray asks you to torch the car, but you can dispose of it in any fashion you desire—ram it, bomb it, shoot it, sink it, or burn it.

RAY MACHOWSKI 4: GONE FISHING

PAYOFF: $15,000
JOB DESCRIPTION: Steal a Police Boat and sink Ray's ratting partner's boat near the lighthouse on Portland Rock.

Follow the red blip on the radar to Asuka's neighborhood in Newport, then head a little south of Asuka's house to the docks where you will find a Police Boat (Predator).

Head to Portland and around to the lighthouse on Portland Rock, located near Portland Beach and the Portland Docks. When you approach the lighthouse, a cinematic will reveal that Ray's partner fishes with grenades—very sportsmanlike! As you approach the boat, it gives chase. Notice the Damage Meter below your Wanted Level—as your bullets make contact with the snitch's boat, the damage becomes more severe.

This chase is much easier than the last boat chase—the Police Boat you're chasing this time is not nearly as fast as the speed boat you pursued last time. However, what it lacks in speed, it makes up for in defense. Ray's partner will occasionally toss an explosive drum out the back of his boat, hoping you'll run into it. The key is to avoid following directly behind him. You have a longer target when you shoot at the side of his boat, anyway. The wake and spray of your target can also camouflage the explosive barrels. Sink the boat and, with it, all the state's evidence and you'll earn $15,000.

70

RAY MACHOWSKI 5: PLASTER BLASTER

PAYOFF: $10,000
JOB DESCRIPTION: Kill the witness getting ready to make a Federal Deposition while he's being moved from Carson General Hospital.

As soon as you exit the park bathrooms, you'll see another Damage Meter below your Wanted Level. This represents the damage inflicted on the ambulance carrying the witness (who's in a full body cast).

Find a car and drive to the red blip on the radar, which tracks the ambulance's movements. There is no time limit involved, but the witness will eventually arrive at the courthouse with his evidence and you'll fail the mission if you don't do something soon.

ESCORT SERVICE

A police escort also protects this important witness. You'll be given an automatic Wanted Level of 2 as soon as you're spotted.

One good sideswipe and the ambulance will eject the witness. The witness's bodycast is remarkably durable and will repel all types of bullets. The new Damage Meter on screen is now that of the witness in the armored bodycast. The only things that will kill this stubborn snitch are your tires or explosions.

Keep in mind that upon ejection of the witness, your Wanted Level increases a notch to 3. You must avoid being annihilated or busted by the cops while getting rid of the witness. The best thing to do is just keep moving and, if your vehicle is about to explode, quickly find the closest replacement.

The armored body cast is also flame-retardant! However, you can park a car on top of the victim and then blow it up to finish him off. Quickly running over the body cast to waste the witness has a lot to do with the weight of the vehicle you're in. If you're in a Banshee, it'll take quite a few passes, but a fire truck may need just one pass. When you destroy the witness for good, you'll earn $10,000!

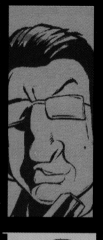

DONALD LOVE

DONALD LOVE 1: LIBERATOR

PAYOFF: $40,000

JOB DESCRIPTION: Ascend the stairs of the Love Media building in Bedford Point and enter the Blue Marker to get work from millionaire, Donald Love.

Donald thanks you for taking care of the morgue party photos as he runs on his treadmill. Then he tells you about an old Asian Gentleman he knows who's being held hostage by some South Americans in Aspatria. They are trying to extort additional funds from him, but he doesn't believe in renegotiation. He wants you to do whatever it takes to rescue this guy.

As you leave the Love Media building, you are instructed to steal a Colombian gang car so you can infiltrate the hideout. Drive north to find a Colombian Cruiser in Fort Staunton.

A red blip on the map will lead you to the old Asian Gentleman. When you reach your destination, you'll see that the area where you need to be is behind the electric gate. The gate will open for the Colombian Cruiser, so drive in and start running over all the gunmen you can before the truck becomes too dangerous to sit in. It only takes them a second to discover you're not one of them before they open fire on you.

BEHIND DOOR NUMBER ONE...

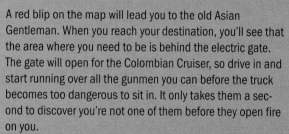

There are a few spare Cruisers in the garages if you are intent on killing them from the safety of a vehicle. The Asian Gentleman is behind one of the closed garage doors and it's not hard to tell which one if you use the radar. Be aware that behind almost every door is an armed Colombian and they will shoot as soon as you open it.

You can run by the doors to trigger them, then toss an explosive into the garage from an angle so they won't shoot you. These doors will not open if you're in a vehicle. Make sure you have your Uzi, AK-47, or handgun in hand and be ready when you open the garage holding the Asian Gentleman. Aim with the R1 button and switch targets with either the L2 or the R2—the Asian man has company and you don't want to take out the wrong guy!

Get the Package

Make sure to pick up the Package by the Colombian Cruiser parked in front of the garages.

The Delivery

Once you have the Asian Gentleman in your custody, take him back to Donald Love's Media Building. He'll follow you into any vehicle you chose to steal. Pull into the Blue Marker in front of the building and stop to let him out. You'll make $40,000! Man, this guy pays well.

Donald Love 2: Waka-Gashira Wipeout

PAYOFF: $30,000	
JOB DESCRIPTION:	Use a Cartel gang car to kill the Yakuza WAKA-gashira, Kenji Kasen, who's at a meeting atop of the multi-story carpark in Newport.

If you just came from Donald's last mission, chances are you drove up to the Love Media building in a Colombian Cruiser. If not, head back to Fort Staunton and steal one. Once you're behind the wheel of this car, a red blip will appear on the radar—follow it to the carpark in Newport.

Newport Carpark

When you drive to the top of the parking garage, Kenji and his men will see you coming. Stay in the car or they'll realize that you're not a Cartel and you'll fail the mission.

Take good care of the Cruiser until you have it on the top of the carpark. There's an astounding amount of firepower on the roof and the car will not last long. You must aim for Kenji—the one with the Blue Arrow over his head—and not worry about anyone else. He's in front of a car near a wall, which makes your angle of approach critical.

Kenji Pancake

Head for the northern end of the lower rooftop, then drive up the ramp to the top. Pull in front of the black limo, between the hood and the dividing wall, then plow over Kenji. If you successfully offed Kenji, you'll see a message that reads; Kenji is tender meat! Get out of Newport and dump the car.

The Great Escape

Descend the opposite ramp and make your way down the multi-story parking lot. You can leave the car in the garage and steal another one if you're afraid it might explode. Head to the next district—Aspatria is close. The mission is complete as you leave Newport and receive $30,000.

DONALD LOVE 3: A DROP IN THE OCEAN

PAYOFF: $10,000
JOB DESCRIPTION: Pick up several packages containing forging plates that were dropped into the bay by a Cessna before anyone else does.

The first thing you need to do after leaving Donald Love's building is find a boat. You have a minute and 34 seconds to do this. There's a speedboat (red blip on the radar) at the Callahan Point dock in Portland.

It won't take long if you head north out of Love Media and take a right in Belleville Park to catch the Callahan Bridge. Keep heading east in Portland and take the first two rights in Trenton. Callahan Point is just around the corner. Make a U-turn into the tunnel and head to the dock.

The speedboat has a Blue Arrow over it. When you enter the boat (Speeder), you'll immediately see the Cessna flying around (yellow blip on the radar).

Follow the plane as often as possible. It will occasionally fly over land, but will always return to drop more packages. The packages appear to be little buoys with lights on top. Run through them to pick them up. Once you've picked up the first package a "Collected" counter will appear below your Wanted Level. Text on the bottom of the screen informs you when the Cessna has dropped another package.

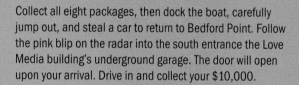

Collect all eight packages, then dock the boat, carefully jump out, and steal a car to return to Bedford Point. Follow the pink blip on the radar into the south entrance the Love Media building's underground garage. The door will open upon your arrival. Drive in and collect your $10,000.

74

STAUNTON ISLAND EXTRA MISSIONS

75

The following jobs are not necessary to complete the game; however, there is money to be made and some interesting folks to meet. You don't want to miss out on it!

CONTINUING WITH DONALD
You can continue to work for Donald Love at this point, but the next Love mission will take you to the last map, Shoreside Vale. You may opt to finish the missions in Staunton Island, as we will in the guide.

KING COURTNEY

KING COURTNEY 1: THE INTERVIEW

PAYOFF: $1,000 PER CHECKPOINT (15 CHECKPOINTS)
JOB DESCRIPTION: Race the Yardies through various checkpoints all over Staunton for a chance to work for King Courtney.

It may be difficult to find a quick car in this neighborhood. You have nothing but time to reach the pink blip on the radar, so do some hunting in the Torrington area. When you're ready, drive into the Blue Marker outside of the Coliseum to begin the race.

Three others have volunteered for the challenge—a Bobcat, a Cheetah, and an Esperanto; a pretty well rounded selection. Look for the pink blips on the radar and try to be the first to each one. As you pass through one, it disappears and another reappears somewhere else on the island.

JUMP THE GUN

Don't wait for the 3-second timer to countdown; in fact, King Courtney admires you for cheating. There are a total of 15 checkpoints and four cars. As long as you pick up more "firsts" than the others, you'll pass the mission. If you fail, you still earn a grand for each checkpoint you passed through first.

If you trash your vehicle, you'll have plenty of time to find another and still win the race. Since your competition has no idea where the next checkpoint will appear, they'll be in as much disarray as you. This buys you lots of time for error. Once you collect more of the 15 checkpoints than any other racer, you win!

KING COURTNEY 2: UZI RIDER

PAYOFF: $10,000
JOB DESCRIPTION: Head over to Hepburn Heights in Portland to whack some Diablos with an Uzi.

You're in control of the Perennial with two Yardies along for the ride. Run over five Diablos on their own turf without ever leaving the vehicle. If you do, the Yardies in the station wagon will attack you!

HEPBURN HEIGHT/PORTLAND

When you make it to Hepburn Heights in Portland, you may notice an increase in patrolling squad cars—and you know by now that if a cop sees you hit someone, there will be hell to pay! The trick is to either not be seen or quickly run over the Diablos walking along the sidewalks, and then immediately head for the Pay 'n' Spray around the corner to shake the cops.

DIABLO-DAY AFTERNOON

The Diablos are the ones with the backward caps, dark shirts, and long shorts. Some of them are holding baseball bats—you can't drive down the sidewalk without hitting one. Try the area where you answered the pay phone to pick up jobs from El Burro.

After taking out five Diablos and choosing to paint or not (depending on your Wanted Level), return the Yardies to Newport in Staunton Island. Follow the pink blip on the radar and stop in the Blue Marker. You'll take home $10,000!

KING COURTNEY 3: GANGCAR ROUND-UP

PAYOFF: $10,000
JOB DESCRIPTION: Steal a Mafia Sentinel, a Yakuza Stinger, and a Diablo Stallion, then drop them off without a scratch at a garage in Newport.

GOTTA BE MINT

If you bang up a car during the delivery, then visit the Pay 'n' Spray—fortunately, it's just a few blocks away from the garage!

Secure appropriate transportation, then follow the pink blip on the radar to the delivery garage.

76

It doesn't matter if you steal one car before another, but they must be in good condition, which makes this otherwise easy job much more challenging. Just take it easy and obey the rules of the road. Watch out for other motorists who have it in for you.

The Yakuza Stinger can be found all over Staunton Island, including Asuka's apartment!

You'll have to travel to Portland for the Mafia Sentinel and the Diablo Stallion; you're not going to find them in this part of town.

You can steal the Mafia Sentinel from the late Salvatore's home in Portland Beach; he won't be needing one anymore.

You already know where the Diablo gang hangs out in Hepburn Heights. If you dent it in Portland, wait to fix it in Staunton Island since the shop is so near the garage. You'll walk away from this job $10,000 richer.

KinG Courtney 4: Kingdom come

Payoff: $10,000
Job Description: Retrieve a vehicle containing a stash in Bedford Point.

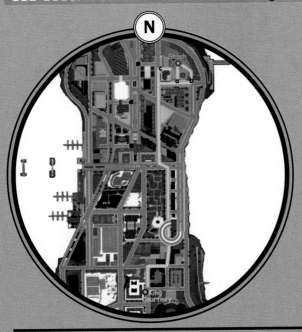

The first challenge in this difficult level is to first reach the parked car in Bedford Point in the time allotted. You have a minute-and-a-half on the clock to do this. Make sure you have a fast car waiting by the phone booth before you take the job, then follow the quickest route on the map we've provided (above).

Lot entrances

There are a few entrances to the parking lot. The quickest into the parking lot are **(C)** & **(B)** on the map. **(A)** leads to a set of stairs and ledge that overlooks the parking lot.

Step into the car with the Blue Arrow over it and you'll find a letter from Catalina. It reads, "I hear you've been a busy boy. Well I've been a busy girl. I think it's time you witnessed the real power of SPANK! Besos y fuderes, Catalina, xxx." Just as soon as you can read the note, SPANKED up suicide bombers begin to run toward the car!

SPANKED UP SUICIDE BOMBERS

The object here is to destroy the three vans that the suicide bombers are pouring out of. These vehicles block the exits—almost.

Don't leave the parking lot and, if you do, don't go far—you don't want to alert the authorities by bringing this mayhem on the streets. As soon as the bomber in the cinematic explodes, back up and spin the car around to quickly drive between the van and the exit (B) on the map. Stop the car just before the sidewalk, then exit the vehicle and fire away.

DESTROYING THE SPANK-MOBILES

Shoot the suicide bombers chasing you through this tunnel. They will continue to pursue you until van is destroyed. Try to shoot them when they're near the van so that the explosion consumes it. The remaining suicide bombers in the parking lot will not follow you out onto the street.

Head around to the stairs—(A) on the map—then go to the top of the ledge and onto the rail. Don't fall into the parking lot! You'll hear and see the bombers at your feet. Take aim at the two remaining vans along the left wall. One is in the distance; the AK-47 works nicely with its long range aiming ability.

Once the vans are toast, you must eliminate the remaining suicide bombers to end the mission. Put some distance between you and them, then throw some Molotov Cocktails or Grenades their way. You just earned another $10,000.

RC TOYZ

RC TOYZ: CASINO CALAMITY

PAYOFF: $1,000 FOR EACH YAKUZA STINGER DESTROYED
JOB DESCRIPTION: Drive the RC cars, rigged with explosives, into the tires or underneath as many Yakuza Stingers as possible in two minutes.

You'll find the Toyz Van, Casino Calamity, in a Torrington parking lot on the block directly across the street and west of the casino. As soon as you take the RC cars out into the streets, you'll see an increase in Yakuza Stingers driving around. Drive the RC car underneath these long white and orange sports cars and press the Circle button to detonate, or run them right into the Yakuza tires to do the job automatically! You earn $1,000 for each Stinger you destroy.

78

Be careful when pulling out of the parking lot with the RC car—it's aimed at the wheels of your Toyz van. Release the X button after a detonation so you won't do yourself in when the next RC car generates!

4X4

4X4 1: A RIDE IN THE PARK

PAYOFF: $30,000
JOB DESCRIPTION: Drive the Landstalker 4x4 to collect 12 checkpoints in two minutes.

You'll find the Landstalker 4x4 in the actual park area of Belleville Park, near the cottage. Collect all 12 checkpoints in any order you like. The two-minute countdown begins when you pass through the first checkpoint. Each one will credit you with 10 extra seconds, giving you time to make it to the next checkpoint, and so on. Don't worry about drowning in the pond—you can drive and wade through the shallow water!

4X4 2: MULTI-STORY MAYHEM

PAYOFF: $30,000
JOB DESCRIPTION: Drive a Stallion to collect 20 checkpoints inside the Trenton carpark in two minutes.

Take a Stallion (they're found all over Staunton Island) to the carpark in Trenton, then exit and re-enter the vehicle to begin this challenge. You may collect the checkpoints in any order. The timer will start immediately.

You'll find four checkpoints on each level of the carpark. The last one is just beyond the ramp in the corner of the top level. Build up enough speed to fly though it!

CHAPTER 4

SHORESIDE VALE

introduction

SHORESIDE VALE HIDEOUT

Once you make it to Shoreside Vale, you can save your progress in Wichita Gardens (when you're not currently engaged in a mission). Follow the green house icon on the radar to the apartment building (see Liberty City Maps just before Chapter 2). As you pull into the driveway, you'll see a row of five garages to your right. The power-ups that you get from collecting Packages will appear here. The triple garage to your left is where you park your car to save it, and the apartment entrance beyond these garages is the door you enter to save your game.

DONALD LOVE

DONALD LOVE 1: GRAND THEFT AERO

PAYOFF: $50,000

JOB DESCRIPTION: Cross the bridge to Shoreside Vale and go to the Francis International Airport to pick up Donald's property from an aircraft fuselage in the customs hangar.

My property will be waiting for you at the customs hangar in the aircraft.

The subway, the tunnel, and a bridge are now all open to Shoreside Vale. If you wish to take the drawbridge, head north along the west coast to the upper deck that circles around to the bridge. This is just west of the Belleville Park (over a corner of it).

DRAWBRIDGE

You may occasionally have to wait for the bridge to lower before crossing. Be patient—the daredevil alternative is deadly.

SHORESIDE VALE

Follow the red blip on the radar to the airport, which looks a lot like LAX airport in L.A. Take a left at the first intersection, then hang the next right and blast through a barricade. No one's there to lift it for you, so just speed right through!

Maintain a westward course until you find the light green hangar (follow the blip). Pull around to the front of the open hangar, then park a few hundred yards away, near a parked airplane. Pull out the sniper rifle and pick off the four members of the Colombian Cartel inside the hangar. You can shoot all of them from outside the hangar by using different vantagepoints. Use the explosive barrels inside to your advantage, as well. Once the threat has been eliminated, enter the Dodo (aircraft with clipped wings) in the hangar.

WHERE'S LOVE'S PACKAGE?

The package is gone! Track down the Colombians and retrieve it. Leave the hangar and inspect the Pan-Lantic construction van with the arrow over it. Hmm... where have you seen one of those before? Ah-ha! Staunton Island, near the hospital!

BACK IN STAUNTON ISLAND

Head back to Staunton Island the same way you came. Follow the pink blip to the Mask Towers construction site in Fort Staunton. Enter the site through the open gate on the east side. Another building is under construction to the north of the blue structure with the Pan-Lantic van and Cartel Cruisers. There's a Colombian inside, in the corner closest to the blue building. Sneak up on him for the kill, then go the upstairs.

82

ENEMY AT THE GATE

Get the Package in the middle of the second floor, then head toward the south corner and use the sniper rifle to dispatch more Colombians in the blue structure below.

Now move on to the blue structure and snipe the two Colombians near the entrance, then carefully make your way around the corner. Two more men await on the second level as you come around the corner.

Walk slowly around the ledge and use the AK-47 or a Molotov Cocktail to eliminate the guy over the wall on the second platform. Continue cautiously to the elevator, prepared for several more kills, then follow the blip to the construction elevator and enter it.

WHO'S DECEIVING WHOM?

A cinematic shows Catalina and her partner in crime, Miguel, getting ready to run with Donald's Package when you surprise them. Catalina shoots her partner as she did you in the beginning of the game. She takes off running and jumps out a window... keep in mind, you are very far from the ground. Asuka doesn't realize that you took out her brother and asks you to drop by later as she whips Miguel, believing he is the killer.

DELIVERY FOR LOVE

As you exit the building, you'll see the Yakuza gang around a Stinger. Take the car—they are still on good terms with you—and bring the Package to Donald Love. Follow the pink blip to the underground garage and collect $50,000! Man, this just keeps getting better.

D-ICE PAGE

After this mission, you get a page to do business with the Jacks, D-Ice. These are extra missions we'll cover once your major contacts have been exhausted—following the ending level, "Exchange."

DONALD LOVE 2: ESCORT SERVICE

PAYOFF: $40,000

JOB DESCRIPTION: Escort Donald's Asian associate to Pike Creek to have his latest acquisition authenticated (the forging plates). Both his associate and the package must remain unharmed.

FINDING JUST THE RIGHT VEHICLE

Get a Barracks OL truck at Phil Cassady's Army Surplus because this mission will have its fair share of collisions. Head for Love Media's underground garage (the red blip). As you pull up to the driveway, you'll see Love's associate in a Securicar.

CLEAN DRIVING RECORD

As you begin your careful pursuit, guarding and blocking attacks for the Asian Gentlemen in the Securicar, you'll quickly realize what a job you have ahead of you. This is no short trip and your target is obeying all the rules of the road! Does he know what game he's in!? Anyway, the Damage Meter beneath your Wanted Level indicates damage to the Securicar. Avoid any action that will increase this level from your own reckless driving.

ROAD TRIP

The first stretch of the trip is relatively painless, if you don't count waiting at red lights. Follow closely behind the Securicar and get used to driving while using the rearview mirror (L2 + R2). This comes in handy as the enemy comes from behind the two of you. Drive with the rearview in short intervals so you don't risk ramming the Securicar yourself. Use both the Handbrake and the regular brake to stop this huge truck in a jiffy.

DRIVE-BY SHOOTING

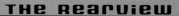

You may find several opportunities in this mission to utilize your drive-by shooting skills. Press and hold either the L2 or R2 button (depending on the side you want to shoot from) plus the Circle button to fire in this deadly manner. It works like a charm when the Cartel drive right next to you.

THE REARVIEW

When you spot someone from behind, cut them off into oncoming traffic, buildings, or whatever will inflict the most damage. Sometimes even just knocking them can send them into a spin to buy you time. With your large uber-truck, destroying many of these vehicles is no big deal.

THE TROUBLE STARTS

Things look pretty grim in the rearview as you turn right into Belleville Park. A Cartel Cruiser is approaching fast. Use the rearview tip mentioned earlier to knock this guy into something other than the Securicar. If he does sneak past you, hit him in the tail section as he comes around to send him into a spin. By Aspatria, you will have picked up another tail.

THE TUNNEL

In Rockford, the Securicar will enter the tunnel in an attempt to make it to Shoreline Vale this way. This is good. You can more easily keep people behind you in a tunnel. The rearview, however, won't help much since the truck is so tall. The Colombian Cruisers can easily jump up onto the sidewalks in the tunnel, so don't get too cocky and forget about that avenue. If you see a Colombian Cruiser begin to burn ahead of you, slam on the brakes! The Securicar is better shielded from this and you need to survive to cover him.

Watch Out for Cops!   **POLICE REPORT**
☐ PRIMARY ☐ SUPP PAGE _____

Be careful not to hit any police cruisers. The last thing you need now is a whole new force against you.

HOME FREE!

Exit the tunnel under the airport and Pike Creek is dead ahead. Another Cartel vehicle attack is imminent and it may even alert the cops, so be on the lookout. You're home free when you see the Plummet billboard on the right side. Your destination, the AMco building, is on the opposite side of the road. When the Securicar pulls into the warehouse safely, you receive your $40,000.

DONALD LOVE 3: DECOY

PAYOFF: $35,000

JOB DESCRIPTION: SWAT teams have cordoned off the area around his associate and the package. Pick up the van and act as a decoy to lead the cops away from the AMco building so he can escape.

Return to the AMco building and have a look around the block. Each road that leads away from the warehouse is littered with cops and SWAT teams in all sorts of vehicles. Block one of the Enforcers with your vehicle to assist in your escape.

As soon as you enter the Securicar, the authorities will be alerted and you'll be tagged with a Wanted Level of 6! That's as high as it goes! Exit the warehouse parking lot before things get too hectic.

You have three minutes on the clock below your Wanted Level. When you see this clock tick down to zero, you win. If not, you fail the mission, most likely because the Securicar could not take the damage or you exited the vehicle for more than 14 seconds. Leaving the main entrance of the parking lot is dangerous.

Once you're out, there's no guaranteed safe place to go. What works well one time, may not be the ticket the next time you attempt this mission.

AIRPORT

It's often helpful to escape downhill since the Securicar is sluggish uphill. Plus, downhill leads to the airport, which is another great place to seek refuge. You can evade the cops on the runway for a long time.

HOSPITAL

Heading for the hospital works well too. You can drive all the way around the hospital, over and over, doing laps to keep the chopper off you and having to deal with only one police vehicle at a time. Since there's only enough room for a couple vehicles between the ledges and the hospital walls, their only option is to hit you from behind—they're not clever enough to attack you head-on.

AND THE WINNER IS...

Perhaps the best place to flee is through the tunnels near the airport—the one you drove through when you protected the Securicar in the last mission. The best thing about the tunnel is that the helicopter can't get to you with its devastating cannon blasts!

DONALD LOVE 3: DECOY

Another good thing about the tunnels is that you know that the cops must be coming from either in front or behind you. Plus, if their vehicles are destroyed, it will take time for more to arrive, since there are only so many entrances. Go to the tunnels and head for Staunton Island. If it gets quiet, then stop and move only when trouble comes from either direction.

REVERSE

Whenever you're in a serious jam, remember you have a reverse gear!

When you survive the three minutes, you will automatically pass the mission and earn $35,000 of Donald Love's money.

LOVE'S DISAPPEARANCE

When you return to Donald Love for more work, you discover that he has disappeared. Head to the Pan-Lantic Construction site to see if you can find some answers from Asuka.

ASUKA KASEN

ASUKA KASEN 1: BAIT

PAYOFF: $35,000

JOB DESCRIPTION: Act as bait for the death squads around Liberty City and get them to follow you to Pike Creek where some Yakuza will be waiting for them.

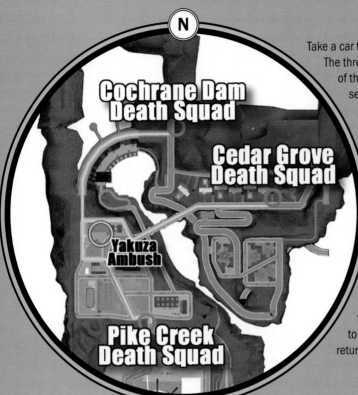

Cochrane Dam Death Squad

Cedar Grove Death Squad

Yakuza Ambush

Pike Creek Death Squad

Take a car to Shoreside Vale, then head to Pike Creek. The three pink blips on the map show the locations of the death squads. The yellow blip is represents your Yakuza allies. You must lead these squads into the lot where the Yakuza gang will open fire on them (you may participate in the carnage). If you try to annihilate them anywhere else but here, you will fail the mission. If a few men escape the firing squad and take off on foot out of the lot, the blip on the radar representing them will turn green and you will be allowed to run them down.

One last thing to remember before taunting them into chasing you and then burning out of the area: Make sure you don't get too far ahead of the pursuers or you're liable to lose them. If you do, they'll turn back and return to their original position.

COCHRANE DAM DEATH SQUAD

Head east across the upper Cochrane Dam road, then spin around when it turns to pavement. You'll see the death squad's car on the side of the road near the blocked off tunnel. Hit the gas and scream back to the west. Continue straight ahead when you reach the paved road near the ambush point and fly into the Yakuza parking lot. Head all the way to the back, then spin around so that the side of your car is facing the entrance. Use the drive-by shooting technique to help the Yakuza team destroy the death squad's car and anyone who exits the vehicle. When the dust settles, pick up their weapons and search for the next group.

PIKE CREEKDEATH SQUAD

Drive south toward the airport, but do not leave Pike Creek. The death squad is on the corner. They will spot you and make chase, so spin the car around 180 degrees and return to the ambush site. Watch the radar and use your rearview to make sure they are following you. Head back the way you came and take them out in the same fashion as before. Pick up their weapons and then begin your pursuit of the last remaining squad.

CEDAR GROVE DEATH SQUAD

Drive to the second from the last house on the left and do a donut in the street. The final death squad is in the driveway of a nearby home. Speed down the street and repeat the same procedure as you have with the others. If your mission does not end after the fourth car is demolished, look on the radar for green blips. If you see any survivors running around, hunt them down and kill them.

ASUKA KASEN 2: ESPRESSO-2-GO

PAYOFF: $40,000
JOB DESCRIPTION: Smash all nine Kappa Coffee Houses, the Cartel's front company for selling SPANK.

You need a swift and heavy vehicle for this mission. Head to the Fort Staunton area to jack a Cartel Cruiser, then visit Asuka in the Mask Towers. After learning the details, jump into the Cruiser and head straight to Shoreside Vale's hospital.

Once you hit the first SPANK stand, the timer begins—similar to the 4x4 missions. Although you need not hit them in any particular order, we've charted out the most sensible course of action.

88

SPANK STAND #1
(SHORESIDE VALE)

Rev up your engine in the parking lot of the Shoreside Vale hospital, then get up some speed, slam into the SPANK stand, and hightail it out of there. The Colombian inside may live through your attack and you don't need any extra damage from his bullets. Follow the route on the map provided here to get to the airport.

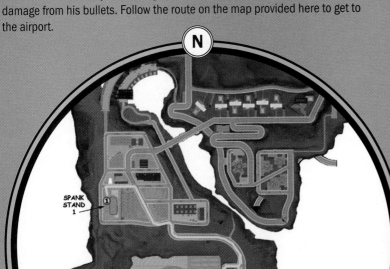

SPANK STAND #2
(SHORESIDE VALE)

Head to the end of the road that runs in front of the airport, then face the stairs that lead up to the fountain and the subway. Wait for traffic to clear, then bolt up the stairs at an angle, heading straight for the SPANK stand. Crush it, then hurry over to the Bridge to Staunton Island.

SPANK STAND #3
(Staunton Island)

Follow the route we've mapped out from the Bridge to the third SPANK stand near the carpark in Newport. Smash it and head south.

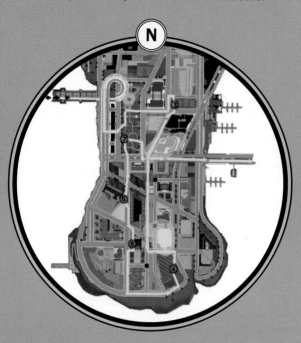

SPANK STAND #4
(Staunton Island)

Head south from Newport to Torrington and find the SPANK stand in the Jefferson Street Credit Union Bank's commons area. Smash it and head south, then west along the southernmost road on the Island. Follow this road, then make the third right and head north to Bedford Point.

SPANK STAND #5
(Staunton Island)

In Bedford Point, you will find the fifth SPANK stand in front of a building blocked by flowerbeds. Drive into the walkway near the building and smack the stand from the side. Move on out of here and head north along the same road.

SPANK STAND #6
(Staunton Island)

The sixth SPANK stand (fourth in Staunton) is in front of the Cathedral of all places! Run directly into the front of it. By now, your vehicle may need to be replaced. Look for something equally as heavy and swift—minivans will work.

SPANK STAND #7 [STAUNTON ISLAND]

From the Cathedral, head due north, then cross the next major road and enter the park through the opening dead ahead. This will almost put you on a perfect trajectory for the last stand in Staunton—up on a hill in the park. Get all the speed you can possibly get on the slick grass and dirt covering the park, then smash the stand and head out of town to Portland via the Callahan Bridge.

SPANK STAND #8 [PORTLAND]

When you arrive in Portland from the bridge, the Portland Harbor is a straight shot (no intersection turns). The eighth SPANK stand is just across the street from the Portland Docks. Run it down and continue in the same direction on this road.

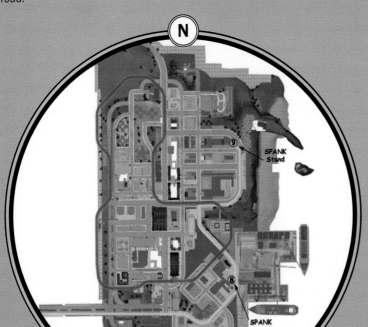

SPANK STAND #9 [PORTLAND]

Head to St. Mark's by making a right turn as you approach the El Train rails above the road. The final SPANK stand is on the beach across the street from the late Salvatore's mansion, just around the corner of a building. Pick up speed and cut sharply to the left as you head around the corner of the building and... SMACK! That's it for the SPANK! Expect 40,000 big ones. SPANK you very much!

> ### D-ICE AND THE JACKS
> After this mission, you'll be paged by D-Ice, the leader of the Jack gang. He wants you to answer the phone in Wichita Gardens, near your Shoreside Vale Hideout.

SHORESIDE | LEVEL I:

ASUKA KASEN 3: S.A.M.

PAYOFF: $45,000

JOB DESCRIPTION: Take a boat out to the runway light buoys and shoot down a plane full of Catalina's poison during its approach to Francis International Airport, then collect the cargo from the debris and stash it.

As soon as you return to the base of the Mask Towers, you'll be given three-and-a-half minutes to find a boat and make it to the buoys near the runway. If you miss the boat, you'll miss the arrival of the plane and fail the mission.

Head toward the red blip on the radar. This will lead you to the west coast of Staunton Island to a pier where you'll find your boat (Reefer) with the Blue Arrow over it. Take the rocket launcher next to the boat, then press the Triangle button to enter the boat safely.

Take the Reefer toward the blue blip on the map. Lightly collide with the buoy with the Blue Arrow over it and a message will appear instructing you to shoot down the aircraft. You can stop here at the buoy and face the east to shoot down the plane; or, if you have time, you can run the boat up the boat ramp near the runway and take aim from the actual runway.

Select the rocket launcher and look to the east. Use the R1 button to enter the rocket launcher's sight mode and fire at the light aircraft as it passes overhead. Wait to shoot until you see the whites of their eyes! Conserve what little ammo you have and make the first shot count.

92

After annihilating the plane, you'll receive a Wanted Level of 4. Drive the boat around the area to pick up the floating packages—just run over them to collect them. If the plane scattered parcels onto the runway, run your boat ashore and begin collecting those smoldering packages, as well. You need to find all eight packages and return them to the construction site.

Since you're so far away from civilization, the first law enforcement to reach you will be a helicopter. Keep moving to avoid the cannons of the chopper. If you have any extra rockets left in the launcher, you can use them to take out the whirlybird, but you'll suffer the consequences of a Wanted Level 5!

ASUKA KASEN 4: RANSOM

Asuka's dead! Miguel has a note on his lifeless body; it reads, "I've got your precious Maria. If you don't want her face to look like she fell out with the butcher, bring $500,000 to the Villa at Cedar Grove."

$500,000 PRIZE

There is no actual mission here; it's simply a cinematic to thicken the plot and to inform you that you must have the amount specified to make an "Exchange" for Maria's life.

RAY MACHOWSKI

RAY MACHOWSKI 1: MARKED MAN

PAYOFF: $20,000 and a Bulletproof Patriot
JOB DESCRIPTION: Take Ray to the airport in time to make his flight and escape the pursuing CIA!

Take off with Ray in the fastest car you can find. You have three minutes to get him to the airport before his flight leaves. The CIA has the bridge under surveillance, so you must find another route across the bay.

The pink blip on the radar represents the drop off point in front of the Francis International Airport. The Callahan Bridge is closed to traffic, so the best route to take is north from the park to Rockford where you pick up the Staunton Island tunnel. Switch to first person view to better avoid the traffic.

When you reach the 'T' in the tunnel, turn left, then left again at the next airport sign (you'll see it just after the Shoreside Vale message appears in the bottom-right corner of the screen).

Emerge from the tunnel, then hang a left at the intersection and stay on this road. Do not turn right toward the runway, because Ray must first check in.

Pull into the Blue Marker and stop. Ray gets out, makes his plane on time, and hands you a nice present—the key to his lock-up.

The clock has now stopped and you're instructed to go to the lock-up. Follow the pink blip on the radar to gradient in Newport. Pull up to the garage door and it will now open for you. You receive a page from Ray as the door is lifting. He says, "Take care of my bullet proof Patriot. See you in Miami." Excellent! A bulletproof car will certainly come in handy. As you enter the lock-up, you'll also receive a flame-thrower, rocket launcher, sniper rifle, and $20,000!

LOCK-OUT GOODIES
This garage is a one-time deal. The pick-ups will be created only once. Park the Patriot in your Hideout garage and save your game!

catalina

catalina 1: the exchange

payoff: $1,000,000

job description: Follow the "C" (for Catalina) on the radar to Cedar Grove to the mansion on the end of the block. With $500,000 in cash pull up into the drive, get out of your vehicle, and enter the Blue Marker at the gates of the Colombian mansion.

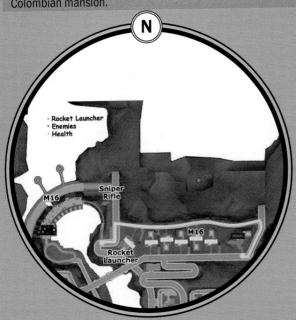

The two Colombian Cartel guards at the gatehouse will take the briefcase, strip you of all your weapons, and escort you into the compound. After handing over the ransom for Maria, Catalina double crosses you and orders her guards to kill you!

hell on wheels

Make sure you've got a fast car—like a Cheetah, Banshee, or an Infernus—waiting for you outside the compound when you escape. There's an abundance of them in this rich neighborhood, so you won't have to look very far.

bulletproof patriot

If you've unlocked the Bulletproof Patriot from completing Ray's mission, then you can use it in this mission. It will provide superb safety from attacks all the way into the dam, until the helicopter takes off and starts bombing you. The Patriot will not repel bombs!

In the opening cinematic, Catalina takes the cash and walks away. As soon as her back is turned, you smash the guard in the face and this is where you take over.

STRIPPED

When you entered the compound, your weapons were taken and you don't have time to search for any sniper rifles, rocket launchers, and such before you find the helicopter. Everything must be picked up from the dead, so killing everyone is necessary to re-arm yourself.

COMPOUND ESCAPE

As soon as you have control, run forward over the guard you just grounded and take his Handgun.

SEVEN MINUTES

You have seven minutes to destroy Catalina's helicopter, not to mention escape the compound and find the aircraft! That's seven minutes to collect weapons, find the helicopter, and destroy it. Move fast!

Keep running toward the gate you entered, then draw the Uzi and hold down the R1 button to aim at the guard on the right. As soon as he goes down, still holding the R1 and ● to continue your deadly stream of ammo, press the L2 button to switch targets. Shoot the Colombian standing by the left side of the gate.

Keep moving to avoid the hail of bullets from all directions. As soon as this guard goes down, run over him to take his AK-47, then whip around and face the mansion to select the next target running toward you. If you run out of Uzi ammo, use your new AK-47.

When he goes down, pick up another weapon at the other end of the gate, then add to your arsenal once again courtesy of the Colombian who was running up behind you. Put away your weapon to run faster toward the mansion, then bust out your AK-47 and waste the Colombian on the mansion balcony. Be frugal with your ammo—it's invaluable.

Put your gun away again and sprint toward the fallen soldier to escape the line of fire and avoid the last gunman on another balcony. Pick up the downed gunman's weapon, then run out toward the empty fountain with AK-47 drawn and turn to shoot the last Colombian on the balcony. Sometimes he won't fall to the ground and you won't be able to pick up his weapon. If you got it... good!

Take the Cartel Cruiser from the garage, along with the Armor power-up, and speed to the gate. When it opens, you can hop out if you have a sports car or Bullet Proof Patriot waiting; if not, keep it.

Dam Fast

As soon as you set foot on the street, Catalina's chopper will fly westward. The red blip on the map tracks her movement. DO NOT head west down this street, it'll take too long to reach the dam.

Instead, head east around the bend and up the hill. Turn left at the next road and tear down the street at full speed, avoiding traffic the best you can. You should have about five-and-a-half minutes remaining at this point. Turn left at the end of this road and follow the curve around to the right.

M-16

As you drive away on the road behind the Colombian mansion, grab the M-16 on the doorstep of the swank pink house two doors down.

Rocket Launcher

There's a Rocket Launcher on the roof of the last swank house to the west end on this block. Use the mound on the east side of the house to run and jump up there.

Dam Infiltration

Stop on the right after you round the bend, then get out of the car, select the Uzi (if you're out of ammo, then use the AK-47), and blast the Colombian standing on the right side of the dual Cartel Cruiser roadblock. When he goes down, pick up his AK-47, then run around the edge of the Cruiser and shoot the Colombian behind the trucks. Pick up his weapon, enter the right Cartel Cruiser (closest to the hill), and burn rubber down the dam road. You should now have five minutes remaining on the clock.

Law Enforcement

Hopefully there are no cops on the road at this point. Sometimes they're around and sometimes they're not. If they see a gunfight, they'll get involved. Not good.

Powerslide the vehicle around before reaching the second blockade, then jump out of the truck and take aim at the Colombian behind the two Cruisers—not the guy standing to the right of them. When you lock on the guy behind the trucks, the Cruisers themselves will take the bullets and explode, killing both guards and saving you time and bullets.

SNIPER RIFLE

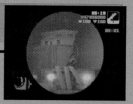

There's a sniper rifle on the cliff before you reach the second block-ade. Use it to snipe as many distant enemies as you can. Make every shot count, you have only five rounds.

Drive your truck up to the destroyed vehicles (depending on how far you stopped from them), then take the two M-16s from the rubble and shoot the Colombian standing on the cargo crates.

If you have any Uzi ammo left, run toward the crates while holding the R1 button to blindly shoot the Colombian near the drums to the right. If he's still alive, come out from behind the crates and shoot him or the drums to finish him. Quickly put the gun away and run up the ramp, then take the gun from the guy on the crates and jump back to where you were for cover. There's a guy up high on the stairs further down to the right who's packing some serious heat.

With your M-16 selected, step back from the crates so you can only see the Colombian on the stairs. Use the R1 button to aim carefully, then use a short burst of fire to shoot him. The gun will recoil as you fire, making this difficult. Practice makes perfect.

Emerge a bit further from behind the crates and look for the Colombian on the ground in front of the blue crates on the left side of the dam. Use the M-16 on him or the oil drums behind him before he advances. You can take this dead Colombian's M-16 before entering the range of the two next round of foes.

Take aim with the M-16 and blast the Colombian on the crates below the next building, then take out the guy on the stairs.

CATALINA'S AIRBORNE!

As you approach the second building, a quick cinematic shows the chopper taking off. You must move even quicker now. You should have at least three minutes remaining to destroy the chopper.

Beware of Big Guns!	POLICE REPORT
	☐ PRIMARY ☐ SUPP PAGE _____

When the helicopter takes flight, watch out! It has bombing capabilities, the likes of which you have not seen before!

As you run to the second building (pick up the M-16 if the guy on the stairs dropped to the ground), a Barracks OL truck tries to run you down. Dart behind the edge of the second building and the dam itself. As it crashes near you, come around the corner and take out the Colombian on the ground near the stairs.

Quickly run up the stairs of the second structure and hide from the helicopter, then grab the M-16. When the helicopter sounds distant, shoot over the wall of the structure to dispatch the the Colombian near the parked Barracks OL.

Remain atop the structure; from this vantage point, you can take out the distant Colombians at the end of the pathway. You can also dodge around the corner of the structure to hide from another chopper bombing.

Stand next to the parked Barrack OL and take out the Colombian on top of the helipad, then take his flame-thrower and duck under the stairs if you hear the helicopter coming. Stay there until the current bombing run has ceased.

Head upstairs and burn or shoot the two Colombians on the right side of the platform. Be careful not to hit Maria who is also standing nearby. Head for the tower in the middle of the platform and shoot the last Colombian in the north-east corner.

Quickly take the rocket launcher from the eastern edge of the platform and use the R1 button to locate the chopper. Take careful aim and wait until it is well within range, because it has only two rockets loaded.

When you down the chopper and Catalina is no more... that's it, you just beat the game! Enjoy the ending and return to Liberty City to keep the madness from ending!

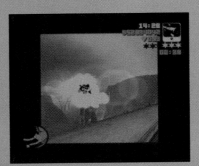

Shoreside Vale!

SHOreSIDe VaLe EXTra MISSIONS

D-ICE 1

D-ICE 1: UZI MONEY

PAYOFF: $10,000

JOB DESCRIPTION: Show the Nines how a real drive-by works.

Don't Make More Enemies!	POLICE REPORT
	☐ PRIMARY ☐ SUPP PAGE _____

Watch your back, there'll be Jacks on the street who will think you're trying to blast them, too!

Ready the Uzi as you enter your vehicle, then look left or right and press ● to fire. Only Drive-by kills with this weapon will count.

You must murder 20 Nines in two-and-a-half minutes. Jump into a car and drive around Wichita Gardens looking for purple jackets.

You can keep driving around the same block and plenty of Nines will continue to appear on the sidewalks. Remember not to run over them, only shooting them with an Uzi from the car will count. Use the forward and reverse to aim while pressing L2 or R2 to look side to side. Watch out for the cops in the area; you don't need to get them involved. If you see a cop, drive around the block so they don't witness any crime.

The Nines will not be passive about their diminishing numbers and will aggressively return fire. Keep in mind that you won't fail the mission if you switch vehicles after yours takes too much damage. Just keep moving! After icing 20 Nines, you will take home $10,000.

D-ICE 2: TOYMINATOR

PAYOFF: $5,000

JOB DESCRIPTION: Find the Toyminator van and wreck all the Nines' armored cars.

Follow the red blip on the radar to D-Ice's apartments in Wichita Gardens. The blue and white Toyminator van is parked in front of a row of garages.

100

If you've already found some of the Toyminator vans throughout Liberty City, then you'll be ready for this mission—it's almost the same drill. The only difference is that you have a limited number of RC cars this time.

Drive the RC car as you would any other vehicle. Press ● to detonate it under an Armored Car or run the RC car into the tires. If you drive the RC car out of range, it will explode. You have four RC cars to destroy three Armored Cars, so you can afford just one error.

The three red blips on the radar represent the three Armored Cars. When an RC car explodes, another is released from your van for another go at it. The Armored Cars are mobile, so you'll rarely find them in the same place each time you play, but they will always be in the same general vicinity. Destroy all three Armored Cars for $5,000.

D-ICE 3: RIGGED TO BLOW

PAYOFF: $20,000
JOB DESCRIPTION: Take D-Ice's car to the garage in St. Mark's (Portland) to have a bomb defused.

Pick up my car and take it over to the garage on St. Marks, a'right yo.

Drive Carefully!   POLICE REPORT
☐ PRIMARY ☐ SUPP   PAGE _____

The clock is ticking and the wiring is hot! One pothole too many and the car, and you, could be blown to pieces!

As soon as you get off the phone with D-Ice, the timer on the clock starts to tick down from six minutes. Quickly enter your vehicle and race toward the red blip on the radar. This will lead you to Wichita Gardens and an apartment building parking lot. You can't miss D-Ice's auto—it's an Infernus with a Blue Arrow hovering over it.

There's a Detonation Meter below your Wanted Level and the timer. As your car experiences jolts, bumps, or collisions, the Detonation Meter will grow. If it fills completely, your remains will be sent to the nearest hospital.

Follow the red blip on the radar to the garage in St. Mark's. The best route to take is through the tunnel, which is quite near. The quickest way to the tunnel is scary, but not harmful at all—if done correctly.

Exit the parking lot and follow the road south. Just past the west end of his apartment building (on your left) before the road turns to the east (left) you can drive down the embankment before the railings along the east curve. Turn the car so that it points directly toward the embankment (west), then coast very slowly over it.

Once you make it to the road below, turn right (north). The tunnel is just down the road a bit on your right. Switch to first person view to better navigate through traffic and read the signs. Continue straight through all the intersections in the tunnel to get to Harwood in Portland. Take a left into St. Mark's and follow the blip to the small garage.

The garage has a narrow door, so be careful pulling it in. Once it's in safely, the bomb will be defused and you'll be instructed to return the car to the same parking lot in Wichita Gardens. If you damaged the car, take it to the Pay 'n' Spray in the Red Light District, then return to D-Ice along the same route to collect your $20,000. Feel free to steal his wheels after collecting your dough.

D-ICE 4: BULLION RUN

PAYOFF: $25,000
JOB DESCRIPTION: Get a car and snatch up 30 pieces of spilled Platinum bullion from crashed a Federal Reserve flight at Francis International, then deliver it to D-Ice's garage within six minutes.

THE TELEPHONE IS RINGING
Answer the pay phone in Wichita Gardens to accept this job from D-Ice.

Follow the pink blip on the radar to Pike Creek. Glowing golden pick-ups are scattered all over the place! The more you pick up, the heavier your vehicle gets, so you must balance load for speed and make several drop offs at the garage. The pink blip on the radar identifies the location of the garage.

Pieces of Platinum do not register on the counter until until you drop them off at the garage. The key to this mission is having the right vehicle and plenty of patience. Heavier vehicles that are made for hauling are better than compact sports cars or sedans. Hoods Rumpo XLs (the dark grey vans) are great for hauling heavy loads. The Colombian Cruisers are also useful in this mission.

HEAVY METAL
With the added load to your vehicle, low speed is not the only hazard in this mission. When you hit anything, the damage inflicted will be twice as bad. Drive cautiously!

With a good truck, you can haul almost 30 Platinum pieces without too much of a slowdown. This is an alternate strategy to making several small shipments to garage. Two deliveries—one large (slow) and one small (quick)—works out very well. When you have a full load, follow the pink blip on the radar to the #2 garage, just east of the Turtle Head warehouse. Complete the mission to earn $25,000.

D-ICE 5: RUMBLE

PAYOFF: $10,000
JOB DESCRIPTION: Battle a gang of Nines with D-Ice's baby brother.

Watch the green blip on the radar to find D-Ice's baby brother. He's waiting in front of a string of garages.

When you meet the Jack, he lays down the rules of the fight club, 'bats only.' No guns and no cars. D-Ice's brother will follow you and enter your vehicle. Follow the green blip on the radar down the dirt road in Wichita Gardens to Shoreside Vale. You'll see a gang of nine Nines (how quaint). Start wailing on them with your bat and don't let up!

It's not a difficult fight if you're persistent—you may not even need the Jack's help. You'll take a beating, but the fight will be over before you know it. Keep beating the ones that are down until others get up. Most of the Nines will go down once and get up again, unless you really let them have it while they're down. After the fight, D-Ice awards you with $10,000.

GRIPPED!
The Patriot parked in this lot is none other than the Shoreside Vale 4x4 challenge. Take the challenge or go back and talk to D-Ice for more work.

4X4

4X4: GRIPPED!

PAYOFF: $30,000

JOB DESCRIPTION: Collect 20 checkpoints in five minutes.

You may collect these checkpoints in any order. Pass through the first one to start the timer. Each checkpoint will add 15 seconds to the clock to help you make it to the next checkpoint.

RC TOYZ

RC TOYZ: RUMPO RUMPAGE

PAYOFF: $1,000 FOR EACH HOOD VAN DESTROYED

JOB DESCRIPTION: Destroy as many Hoods Rumpo XLs as you can in two minutes.

In Wichita Gardens, behind your Hideout apartment in a corner behind two billboards is the Toyminator van: Rumpo Rampage. Once you enter the van you will be given two minutes to blow up as many Hoods Rumpo XLs as possible. The Hood vans are dark grey. Simply drive the RC Cars out onto any surrounding street and begin the mayhem!

PACKAGE

Don't forget to pick up the hidden Package behind the Toyz van!

104

CHAPTER

5

North

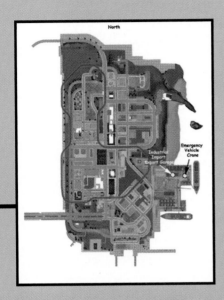

Industrial
Import
Export Garage

Emergency
Vehicle
Crane

secrets

HOOKER TRICK

Pull up to any Hooker (pink or brown outfits) on any street so that she is on the passenger's side of the vehicle and wait for her to walk up to the window and talk to you (she'll only appear to talk). After a moment she'll enter the vehicle. At this time, pull into the closest alleyway (if that doesn't work, try a more secluded alley). When the vehicle starts to rock, you'll gain health. If your health is below 100 points, this trick can take it up to a maximum of 125. The trade-off is that for every two points of health you gain, you lose one dollar—not a bad deal!

GOTTA HAVE THE RIGHT WHEELS

Hookers won't get into just any vehicle. They seem to shy away from Taxis, vans, and law enforcement vehicles.

As the rocking speeds up to a faster tempo, you receive health at a faster rate. This is also when the Hooker is about to bail on you. After approximately 40 points of extra health is given, the Hooker will exit the vehicle to stretch her legs. To continue this cheat when she bails, exit the vehicle when she does, and then quickly re-enter the vehicle while she is still near the car. This will entice her to re-enter the vehicle and do some more rock'n!

Move the car while she is still in the vehicle and you'll receive the final few points of health, then stop again for the cheat to continue. Now you don't even have to get in and out of the vehicle and risk losing the girl. You can continue this process until you reach the 125 maximum health limit.

VEHICLE MISSIONS

When you enter a Taxi, Fire Truck, Police Car, Ambulance, Mafia Car, Enforcer, or a Rhino (tank), you can pick up missions that relate to that vehicle by pressing the R3 button (press down on the right Analog Control Stick). The following section discusses the details of those jobs and what you can earn for completing enough of the individual missions. These missions are tracked on the In-game Stats Menu.

Penalty for Early Withdrawl	POLICE REPORT
	☐ PRIMARY ☐ SUPP PAGE _____

Exit any of the vehicles during a mission and the mission will end, except for the Vigilante missions where you are given 60 seconds to re-enter a law enforcement vehicle.

TAXI MISSIONS

DETAILS

Pick up a pedestrian with a Blue Arrow overhead, then drive them to the specified location before the time runs out. The clock is located below your Wanted Level. When you pick up the fare, a destination message will appear on the bottom of the screen. The pink blip on the radar identifies your intended location. A Blue Marker appears at the actual destination. Stop there to let the passenger out and get paid, then quickly move on to the next passenger, which will appear as a green blip on the radar.

PAYOFF

The fares you make are yours to keep. Complete 100 taxi missions (not necessarily in a row) and a new Borgnine Taxi is created in Harwood.

AMBULANCE MISSIONS

DETAILS

Drive patients to the nearest hospital... carefully. If the ride is too hazardous, they are likely to find a different way to the hospital. Follow the pink blip on the radar to the bleeding individual with the Blue Arrow overhead. Once the victim is in the Ambulance, rush them to the hospital, which will appear on the radar as another pink blip. Stop in the Blue Marker in front of hospital admittance, then pick up the next wounded individual (check the radar again). Use the Siren (tap L1) to make some caring citizens move to the side of the road. Ambulance missions are measured in levels; the higher the level, the more pickups in a single outing. Time is added to your total for each person picked up.

PAYOFF

If you save 50 pedestrians, Health power-ups will be created at your Hideouts. Save 100 pedestrians and Adrenaline is created at the Hideouts. If you complete Ambulance Level 16, then Infinite Run is awarded, enabling you to run without tiring!

Fire-truck missions

Details

Steal a Fire-truck, then press the R3 button to accept the challenge. You are immediately given a specified amount of time on the clock below the Wanted Level to extinguish the fire. Follow the red blip on the radar to the specified location. Press the L1 button to turn on the sirens and hopefully persude vehicles to clear out of your way; if they don't, then just plow through them. You need to extinguish only the specified fire, it doesn't matter if you create your own in the process! You will always find a burning vehicle at the fire locations. Press ● as you drive toward it and aim the stream of water at the fire. The button is analog so the harder you press, the further the water shoots. Once the flames are out, move on to the next fire.

Payoff

You double the money earned with each consecutive fire extinguished in a single mission. Put out 30 fires in each area of town (covering all three districts) to get the Flame-thrower at your Hideout. This weapon will not be unlocked by collecting Hidden Packages.

Vigilante missions

Details

Enter a Police Car, FBI Car, Enforcer, or the Rhino and press the R3 button to activate the Vigilante missions. As always the case when driving an emergency vehicle mission, using the siren will usually make vehicles pull over and get out of your way. Also, listen to the dispatch radio as well as watching the radar to find the location of the target.

RHINO CONTROLS
If you're lucky enough to snag a tank from a Wanted Level 6 frenzy, press ● to fire and spin the turret with the Right Analog Joystick.

Now the shoe is on the other foot! This time, you're the one chasing the bad guys! Culprits race around in their vehicles (green blips on the radar). Chase them down and run 'em off the road or just do your best to make them stop. If the wreck doesn't kill them, they'll jump out and take off on foot. Run them over or cap 'em, whichever way works best for you. If you get out of the vehicle, you have 60 seconds to return to it or another law enforcement vehicle. There are no arrests. You're out to eliminate the bad guys.

Payoff

Kill 40 criminals in each area of town in all three districts to create Police Bribe power-ups at the Hideouts. Two are awarded for each district.

EMERGENCY VEHICLE CRANE

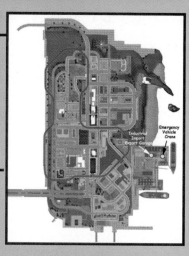

Head to the ship closest to Portland Beach at the Portland Docks. Look for the hanging crane magnet near the stack of storage containers beside the ship. Drive any of the listed emergency vehicles underneath the magnet and step out of the vehicle. The magnet will pick up the vehicle and deliver it to the ship.

The vehicles that need to be delivered are an Ambulance, Fire-truck, Police Car, Enforcer, Barracks OL, Rhino (Tank), and an FBI Car.

PAYOFF

You'll be awarded $1,500 per vehicle–it will only accept one of each of the specified vehicles. When all seven vehicles are delivered you'll, receive $200,000 plus seven GTA pick-ups for each of the vehicles collected. Return to these GTA pick-ups to order the vehicle of your choice.

INDUSTRIAL IMPORT EXPORT GARAGE

The Industrial Import Export Garage is due west of the Emergency Vehicle Crane. Look for the two-toned blue garage door with a car list posted to the left of it. Deliver the following cars: Securicar, Moonbeam, Coach, Flatbed, Linerunner, Trashmaster, Patriot, Mr. Whoopee, Blista, Mule, Yankee, Bobcat, Dodo (airplane with clipped wings), Bus, Rumpo, and the Pony.

HARD-TO-FIND VEHICLES

Having difficulty finding the Mr. Whoopee ice cream truck or the Trashmaster? Take up some Vigilante or Fire-truck missions and they'll appear. Make sure you preserve them when you find them. All these cars randomly generate. The Dodo will turn up when you start taking jobs from Donald Love.

PAYOFF

Deliver all of the vehicles on the list to receive $200,000, plus 16 GTA pick-ups for each of the vehicles collected. You can then walk into the icons to have the car of your choice delivered for your use during missions.

SUBURBAN IMPORT EXPORT GARAGE

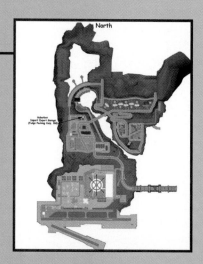

This is located in Shoreside Vale on a corner in Cochrane Dam between the upper road along the dam and the bridge that takes you to Cedar Grove. The garage is part of the Fudge Packing Corp. It has a car list posted to the left of the rusty-red garage door. Deliver the following list of cars: Sentinel, Cheetah, Banshee, Stinger, Infernus, Esperanto, Kuruma, Stretch, Perennial, Landstalker, Manana, Idaho, Stallion, Taxi, Cabbie, and a BF Injection.

PAYOFF

When you deliver all the cars on the list, you get $200,000 and 16 GTA pick-ups. These icons have the label of the car hovering over them. Enter the garage and walk into the correct icon to order that car. Walk out of the garage and the car will be delivered. Enter the garage and drive off in that car for each of the vehicles collected.

BULLET PROOF PATRIOT

After completing Ray Machowski's level, Ray's lock up is opened in Newport. You'll find a Bulletproof Patriot, Flame-thrower, Rocket Launcher, and Sniper Rifle—plus $20,000! These pick-ups will be created only once.

JOEY'S BF INJECTION

After completing Asuka mission 1 (Sayonara Salvatore), Joey's BF Injection is created at Misty's Flat in Hepburn Heights near the El Burro phone. Afterward, these buggies will begin to randomly appear just as the other vehicles do.

HIDDEN PACKAGES

There are 100 Hidden Packages throughout Liberty City and some of them are very difficult to find (see Maps on pages 110-112 for locations). There are different ways to get these hard-to-get Packages. Since you can't fly, you must find stairs, ramps, dirt mounds, or jump from higher structures—like building rooftops or El Train tracks. You receive $1,000 for every Package you find; for every 10 collected, a power-up appears and regenerates at your Hideouts. Use the following list with the maps and half of the challenge is over.

POWER-UP PRIZES

Packages Collected	Power-up Created in Hideout(s)
10	Handgun
20	Uzi
30	Armor
40	Shotgun
50	Grenades
60	Molotovs
70	AK-47
80	Sniper Rifle
90	M-16
100	Rocket Launcher + $1,000,000 cash bonus

HIDEOUT BODY SHOP & EXTRA POWER-UPS

Every time you park a damaged car in the Hideout garage and save your game, the car will be repaired, good as new, when you return! After finding quantities of Hidden Packages, weapons will appear at your Hideout. Oftentimes, you can get double the ammo by taking the weapons before and after you make a save.

PORTLAND

1 Harwood; drive north to the end of the path.

2 Harwood, on roof of Head Radio station. Jump from El Train tracks.

3 St. Mark's, on top of the AMco Gas Station building. Walk the street walls and jump from one rooftop to the next.

4 St. Marks, inside Easy Credit Autos. Break glass.

5 Portland Beach, Salvatore's Mansion, north ledge.

6 On a beach ledge below Salvatore's back balcony.

7 Hepburn Heights Towers, behind building as far as you can go.

8 Hepburn Heights Towers, in parking lot island near El Burro phone.

9 Hepburn Heights, between trees.

10 St. Mark's, one block due south from AMco Gas Station, in small parking lot. Enter driveway in back of building.

11 St. Mark's, building facing large potholes. Climb rubble around back.

12 St. Mark's Park, all the way to the back wall.

13 Red Light District. Take stairs to roof of Luigi's Sex Club 7 and jump to next roof west.

14 Red Light District. Take stairs to roof of Luigi's Sex Club 7.

15 Red Light District, rooftop opposite across from Joey's Sex Club; stairs in the alley.

16 Chinatown Subway, near bathrooms on the middle level.

17 Red Light District. Smash the glass of the Rush Construction Company building.

18 St. Marks, long sloping alleyway in back yard.

19 St. Mark's, tramp tunnel. Enter near Super Save or 8-Ball's.

20 Portland View, on top of Supasave. Jump down from the El Train track onto rooftops.

21 Chinatown Market, alley behind Hong Hung Inc.

22 Chinatown rooftop. Use stairs.

23 Chinatown, alleyway behind Roast Peking Duck.

24 Trenton, inside the gates and behind the Bitch 'n' Dog Food Factory.

25 Trenton, roof of Liberty Pharmaceuticals.

26 Portland Docks rooftop. Use stairs near Colombian ship and jump to the awning of the next building.

27 Trenton, in yard via an alley ramp and Police Bribe.

28 Trenton, in front of Joey's Garage and behind fence.

29 Callahan Point Power Plant, behind concrete fence facing Saw Mill.

30 Trenton Sawmill rooftop. Jump dirt mound in a car behind the mill.

31 Callahan Point, behind the Turtle Head Fish Co. Use a Belly-Up truck or the Trashmaster to enter.

32 Atlantic Quays, at the end of the long paved pier.

33 Island south of Portland. Use boat to dock on rocks.

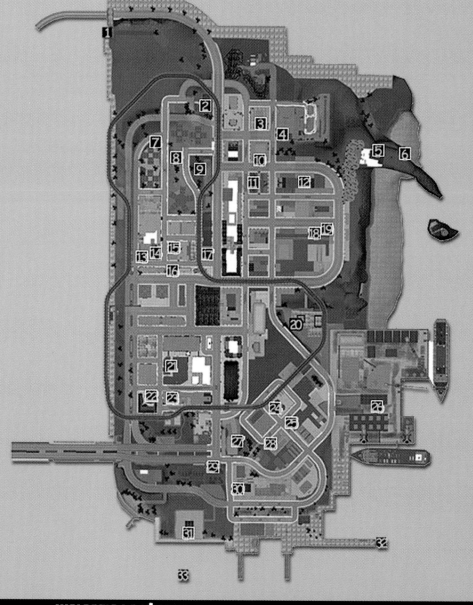

staunton island

36 packages

34	Army surplus, corner between garage and sea wall.
35	Coliseum, behind RockStar billboards.
36	On top of hospital overhang, east of entrance.
37	Stadium entrance.
38	East side of university, facing street.
39	Construction site, small building, second level, inside room.
40	On top of small bridge. Jump on girders and walk up.
41	In Colombian Garage where you saved the OOG.
42	Construction site, on the ground in a corner.
43	Connecting alley to 8-Ball's in a garage next to carpark.
44	Multi-story carpark, second floor corner, near ramp.
45	Alleyway south of Coliseum, Uncle BJ's Deli & Grocery.
46	Jump off (in car) of suburban curvy bridge onto rooftop.
47	Under road tunnel, lower shoreline road, in corner near ramp.
48	Basketball court.
49	Staunton to Shoreside bridge in center median of drawbridge.
50	Under park bridge.
51	End of third south dock, on Pier north of Callahan Bridge.
52	Newport, L-shaped alleyway near Callahan Bridge.

53	Museum, top of stairs.
54	Pier, south of Callahan Bridge. Jump up, away from water, to grab hovering package.
55	Behind Police station, in parking lot.
56	Newport, lower pathway to Police station, in parking nook.
57	Behind the Church.
58	End of Alleyway.
59	Underground AMco parking garage, near elevator.
60	Take ground level Fire Exit doorway to very top of AMco rooftop (multi-leveled).
61	Bedford point, upstairs in smashable glass building.
62	Doorway facing intersection.
63	On roof in projects area.
64	Behind rocks on pavement before Pier.
65	Behind building in projects area.
66	Underground carpark.
67	On top of pedestrian walkway.
68	Behind star statue logo.
69	On top of Kenji's casino on helipad; take stairs.

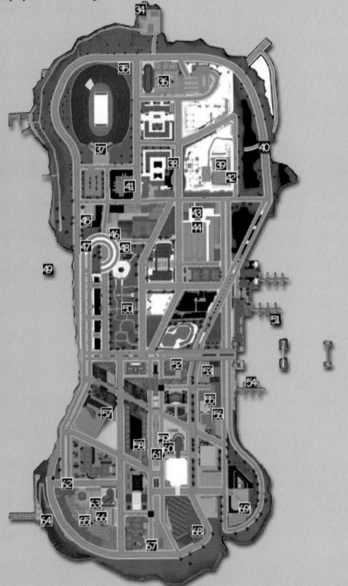

31 PACKAGES

70	West dam dome.
71	East dam dome.
72	First dam Tower.
73	Lower dam, "Exchange" helipad.
74	Behind boulder, corner of dam building and canyon wall.
75	Behind the furthest west swank house.
76	Front porch of third furthest west swank house.
77	Front porch of fourth furthest west swank house.
78	Colombian mansion, in swimming pool.
79	Shoreside Vale, picnic tables.
80	Fudge Packing Factory; walk concrete walls, jump down to rooftop, drop into fenced-in area.
81	Cedar Grove, in overpass tunnel behind Hideout.
82	Behind Police station, on roof.
83	Pike Creek, behind building amongst oil drums.
84	Behind Hideout, billboard, and Toyz Van.

85	Wichita Gardens, entrance to apartments.
86	Wichita Gardens, in between apartment buildings.
87	Pike Creek, on blue container, in lot east of hospital.
88	Behind hospital.
89	Rooftop; use stairs on opposite building, jump to the awning of the next.
90	Pike Creek between back wall and Turtle Head storage garage.
91	Wichita Gardens, under twisted wooden bridge.
92	Airport, across from parking lot.
93	Airport, under wing of plane near hangars.
94	Airport, on ground next to Dome.
95	Airport, under plane.
96	In front of Airport, behind billboards.
97	Subway, lowest level.
98	Airport, on helipad.
99	Airport runway, lower ledge near water.
100	Airport, end of a runway, lower ledge.

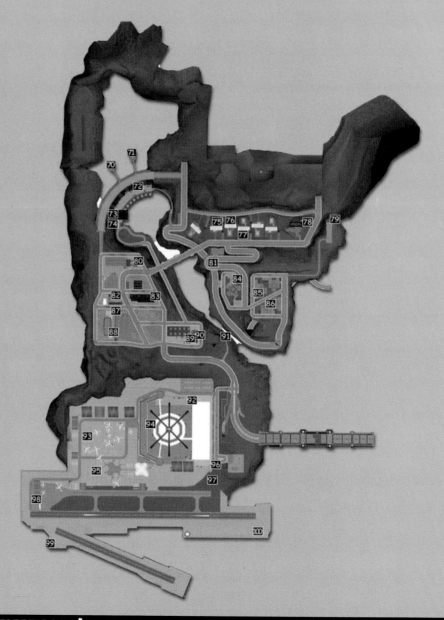